CROCHET &
Ultimate Poncho Book™

Introduction

Discover how liberating wearing a poncho can be! Go from daytime casual by wearing it over jeans to nighttime glamour when wearing it over a sleek and elegant evening dress. This fun and versatile fashion trend is being spotted everywhere from high society galas and penthouse parties to city streets and beaches at sunset.

With the variety of styles in this incredible collection of 50 fabulous ponchos, you can create a look that's perfect for any occasion, from sporty and playful to dazzling and sophisticated. Stitched in a tantalizing mix of yarns and threads, these sensational designs feature a delicious blend of colors, textures and weights for year-round wear.

Whether you're off for a romantic dinner for two or hiking in the hills, the Ultimate Poncho Book has got you covered. With designs for babies, kids, teens and adults, this super collection of creative cover-ups will delight fashion divas of all ages and tastes with attention-getting ponchos that combine the best of today's contemporary styles.

Contents

Evening Out

Design by George Shaheen

SKILL LEVEL
■■□□ EASY

FINISHED SIZE
Woman's small/medium (large/extra-large) Instructions are given for smallest size, with larger sizes in parentheses. When only 1 number is given, it applies to all sizes.

FINISHED MEASUREMENTS
Approx 38 x 19 (46 x 20) inches

MATERIALS
❑ Glitterspun 60 percent acrylic/27 percent cupro/13 percent acrylic worsted weight yarn from Lion Brand (115 yds/50 g per ball): 6 (8) balls bronze #135
❑ Size 11 (8mm) 36-circular needle
❑ Size 15 (10mm) 36-circular needle or size needed to obtain gauge
❑ Crochet hook size H/8 (5mm)
❑ 1 (¾ inch) black button
❑ Sewing needle and matching thread

GAUGE
14 sts = 4 inches/10cm in pat st before blocking
To save time, take time to check gauge.

PATTERN NOTES
Circular needle is used to accommodate large number of sts. Do not join; work in rows.

When measuring, be sure piece is flat and not stretched, as this pattern tends to grow vertically and shrink horizontally.

PONCHO
With larger needle, cast on 146 (178) sts.

Row 1 (WS): P1, *p3tog, work (k1, p1, k1) in next st; rep from * to last st, p1.

Rows 2 and 4: Purl.
Row 3: P1, *work (k1, p1, k1) in next st, p3tog; rep from * to last st, p1.
Rep Rows 1–4 until piece measures approx 16 (17) inches, ending with Row 2.
Change to smaller needles.

Shape neck
Row 1: P1, [work (k1, p1, k1) in next st, p3tog] 9 (10) times, *work (k1, p1, k1) in next st, p3tog, p1, p3tog, work (k1, p1, k1) in next st, p3tog; rep from * 5 (7) times, [work (k1, p1, k1) in next st, p3tog] 9 (10) times, p1–134 (162) sts.
Row 2, 4 and 6: Purl.
Row 3: P39 (43), *p2tog, p3; rep from * 11 (15) times, p35 (39)–122 (146) sts.
Row 5: P37 (41), *p2tog, p2; rep from * 11 (15) times, p37 (41)–110 (130) sts.
Bind off as follows: P38 (42), *p2tog, p1, rep from * 11 (15) times, p36 (40).
Block piece to measure 38 x 19 inches (46 x 20 inches).

FRINGE
Cut strands of yarn, each 18 inches long; use 4 strands for each knot.
Holding 4 of strands for 1 knot tog,

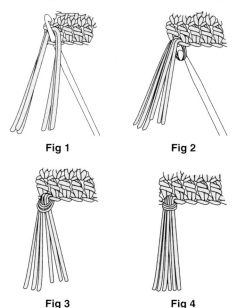

Fig 1   Fig 2

Fig 3   Fig 4

fold group in half. With RS of poncho facing and crochet hook, draw folded end through space or stitch from RS to WS. (Figs. 1 and 2), pull loose ends through folded section (Fig. 3) and draw knot up firmly (Fig 4).
Tie 1 knot in every 4th st across bottom edge and every 5th row across side edges. Tie 2 knots in each corner. On 3rd row of knots, do not tie a knot on either end of fringe.
Row 2: With RS facing, working from left to right, take half the strands of 1 knot and half the strands in the knot next to it, tie group tog in an overhand knot. (Fig. 5).

Fig 5

Row 3: Tie another row of knots, using alternate strands of yarn from previous row. (Fig. 6)

Fig 6

ASSEMBLY
Lay piece flat with WS facing. Referring to photo, fold right-hand edge to meet left-hand edge. Sew upper left back corner over upper left front corner, overlapping 2 (2½) inches at neck edge and having tip of back corner 1 inch from side edge.
Sew button through all layers of corner closure.❑❑

Pistachio Lace-Up

Design by Joy Prescott

SKILL LEVEL
■■■□ INTERMEDIATE

FINISHED SIZES
Ladies 34–40-inch bust (small/medium); Ladies 44–50-inch bust (large/X-large)
Pattern is written for small/medium size with larger sizes in [ ].

FINISHED GARMENT MEASUREMENT
32½–40½ [39½–45] inches

MATERIALS
- ❑ Bouclé or rickrack fine (sport) weight yarn: 500 [675] yds green
- ❑ Medium (worsted) weight yarn: 1 oz/50 yds/28g gray
- ❑ Size 10 crochet cotton thread: 110 [135] yds green
- ❑ Sizes G/6/4mm and I/9/5.5mm crochet hooks or size needed to obtain gauge
- ❑ Size 6/1.80mm steel crochet hook
- ❑ Sewing needle
- ❑ Thread
- ❑ 2 glass ½-inch-wide beads

GAUGE
Size I hook and sport yarn:
6 (ch 3, 3 dc) sts = 7 inches; 6 rows = 4½ inches
Take time to check gauge.

INSTRUCTIONS
SIDE
Make 2.
Row 1: Starting at elbow, with I hook and sport yarn, ch 4, 3 dc in 4th ch from hook, turn. *(1 pattern st made)*

Row 2: Ch 4, 3 dc in 4th ch from hook, sk next 3 sts, sl st in top of ch-3, ch 3, 3 dc in same st, turn. *(2 pattern sts)*
Row 3: Ch 4, 3 dc in 4th ch from hook, [sk next 3 sts, sl st in top of next ch-3, ch 3, 3 dc in same st] across, turn. *(3 pattern sts)*
Rows 4–27 [33]: Rep row 3. At end of last row, fasten off.
Using sewing thread and needle, sew back seam according to illustration.

BOTTOM TRIM
With size 6 hook and size 10 thread, join with sc in lower left front corner, sc around bottom edge, working 5 sc in end of each row across to bottom edge of right front corner. Fasten off.

FRINGE
Cut 108 [132] 23-inch lengths of sport yarn. Fold one strand in half, insert hook in st, pull fold through st, pull ends through fold.

Evenly space fringe around bottom edge.

FRONT TRIM
With size G hook and gray, join with sl st in lower right front corner, ch 1, sc in same sp, working up front opening, [5 sc between points, (sc, ch 3, sc) in each point] across front, evenly sp sc across back neck edge, rep between [ ] down other side of Front. Fasten off.

TIES
With size G hook and gray, leaving 6-inch end, ch 250 [275]. Leaving 6-inch end, fasten off.
Beg at bottom edge and ending at top edge, thread tie back and forth across front through ch-3 spaces on points.
Place a bead on each end of yarn. Tie knot in each end to secure bead.❑❑

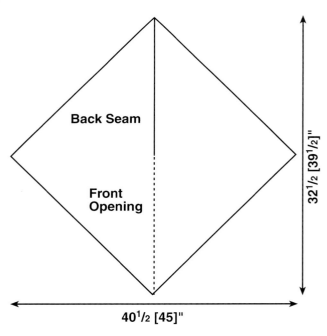

Summer Breeze

Design by Eleanor Shnier

SKILL LEVEL
 BEGINNER

FINISHED SIZE
One size fits most

MATERIALS
❑ Lion Brand Cotton-Ease medium (worsted) weight yarn:

  10½ oz/621 yds/300g #148 popsicle blue
❑ Size P/15/10mm crochet hook or size needed to obtain gauge

GAUGE
3 sc = 1 inch, 3 sc rows = 1 inch
Take time to check gauge.

INSTRUCTIONS
Rnd 1: Ch 105, sl st in first ch to form ring being careful not to twist ch, ch 1, sc in each ch around, **do not join**, mark first st of each rnd. *(105 sc made)*

Rnds 2–4: Sc in each st around.

Rnd 5: Ch 3 *(counts as first dc,)* 2 dc in same st, ch 3, sk next 2 sts, [3 dc in next st, ch 3, sk next 2 sts] around, join with sl st in 3rd ch of beg ch-3. *(35 dc-groups)*

Rnds 6–22: Sl st in each of next 2 sts, (sl st, ch 3, 2 dc) in next ch sp, ch 3, [3 dc in next ch sp, ch 3] around, join.

Rnd 23: Ch 1, [sc in sp between sts, ch 1] around with 2 sc in each ch sp, join with sl st in first sc.

Rnd 24: Ch 1, sc in each st and ch around, join. Fasten off.

FRINGE
Cut three strands each 18 inches long. Hold all strands tog, fold in half, insert hook in st, pull fold through st, pull ends through fold. Pull to tighten.
Fringe around bottom edge, 2 inches apart, in sts. Trim ends.❑❑

Floating Coasters

Design by George Shaheen

SKILL LEVEL
■■□□ EASY

FINISHED SIZES
Woman's small/medium (large/extra-large) Instructions are given for smallest size, with larger sizes in parentheses. When only 1 number is given, it applies to all sizes.

MATERIALS
- Color Waves 83 percent acrylic/17 percent polyester bulky weight yarn from Lion Brand (3 oz/125 yds per skein):
   2 skeins Caribbean #307
- Size 13 (9mm) straight needles
- Size 15 (10mm) straight needles or size needed to obtain gauge

5 BULKY

GAUGE
4 reps = 5½ inches; 8 rows = 2½ inches in pat st
To save time, take time to check gauge.

PANEL
Make 2.
With larger needles, cast on 74 (82) sts.
Row 1 (WS): P1, *yo, p4tog; rep from * to last st, p1–38 (42) sts.
Row 2 (RS): K2, *work (k1, yo, k1) in next st, k1; rep from * across–74 (82) sts.
Row 3: P1, *p4tog, yo; rep from * to last st, p1–38 (42) sts.
Row 4: K1,* work (k1, yo, k1) in next st, k1; rep from * to last st, k1–74 (82) sts.
[Rep Rows 1–4] 6 times more.
Change to smaller needles.
Next row: P1, *yo, [p2tog] twice; rep from * to last st, p1–56 (62) sts.
Knit 6 rows.
Bind off.

ASSEMBLY
Block each panel to measure 25 (28) x 11 inches.
Referring to Fig. 1, sew panels tog.□□

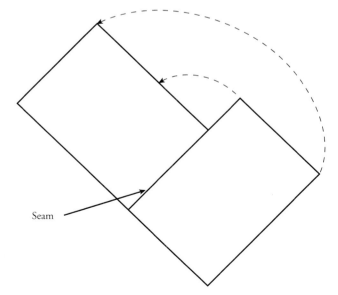

Seam

Fig. 1

CROCHET

Evening Capelet & Pouch

Design by Ann Parnell

SKILL LEVEL
■■■□ INTERMEDIATE

FINISHED SIZES
Capelet: Instructions are given for small/medium, changes for large/extra large are in [ ]
Pouch: 4 x 5 inches, not including drawstrings

MATERIALS FOR CAPELET
- ❑ Metallic crochet thread size 10: 800 yds each ecru and gold
- ❑ Size H/8/5mm double-ended hook or hook size needed to obtain gauge
- ❑ Tapestry needle

MATERIALS FOR POUCH
- ❑ Metallic crochet thread size 10: 200 yds each ecru and gold;
- ❑ Size H/8/5.5mm double-ended crochet hook or hook size needed to obtain gauge
- ❑ Size E/4/3.5mm crochet hook
- ❑ Tapestry needle
- ❑ 13½ inch circle of lightweight fabric (optional)

GAUGE
Size H hook and 2 strands held tog: 5 shells = 3 inches, 6 shell rows = 1 inch
Take time to check gauge.

PATTERN NOTES
Use 2 strands same color thread held together unless otherwise stated.
To **pull up lp**, insert hook in vertical bar, yo, pull lp through leaving lp on hook.
When **picking up lps,** leave all lps on hook unless otherwise stated.
To **turn,** rotate hook 180 degrees and slide all lps to opposite end. Do not turn unless otherwise stated.
To **work lps off hook when adding a new color,** with new color, place sl knot on hook, pull sp knot through first lp on hook, [yo, pull through 2 lps on hook] across.
To **work lps off with color already in use,** pick up color from row below, yo, pull through 1 lp on hook, [yo, pull through 2 lps on hook] across. You will always have 1 lp left on your hook at the end after working lps off, this will be the first st of the next row.

INSTRUCTIONS
CAPELET
Row 1: With ecru, ch 63, pull up lp in 2nd ch from hook (see Pattern Notes), pull up lp in each ch across, turn. (63 lps on hook)

Row 2: With gold, pull through first lp on hook, ch 1, yo, pull through 4 lps on hook (completes a ch- 2 and a shell), *ch 2, yo, pull through 4 lps on hook, (completes a ch-3 and a shell); rep from * across to last 6 lps on hook, ch 1; for **neck ribbing,** [yo, pull through 2 lps on hook] 5 times, **do not turn.** (19 shells)

Row 3: Sk first vertical bar, pull up lp under each of next 5 horizontal bars (see illustration), sk next shell, [pull up lp in top strand of next 3 chs, sk next shell] across to last ch sp, pull up lp in top strand of last 2 chs, turn. (62 lps on hook)

Horizontal Bar

Row 4: With ecru, pull through first lp on hook; for **neck ribbing,** [yo, pull through 2 lps on hook] 5 times, *ch 2, yo, pull through 4 lps on hook (completes a ch-3 and a shell); rep from *across to last 3 lps on hook, ch 2, yo, pull through last 3 lps on hook (completes a ch-3 and a shell), **do not turn.**

Row 5: Ch 1, sk first shell, [pull up lp in top strand each of next 3 chs] across to last 5 horizontal bars, pull up lp under each of last 5 horizontal bars, turn. (63 lps on hook)

Rows 6–340 [6–376]: Rep rows 2–5 consecutively, ending with row 4. At end of last row, leaving long end for sewing, fasten off. Matching sts, sew first and last rows tog.

Optional: Capelet is designed to have a low neckline. If a tighter neckline is desired, make a drawstring as follows: with 1 strand each color held tog, ch 240 or to desired length, sl st in 2nd ch from hook and in each ch across. Fasten off.
Weave through ends of rows at top of neck ribbing. Pull up to gather and tie ends into a bow.

POUCH
Row 1: With double-ended hook and ecru, ch 30, pull up lp in 2nd ch from hook, pull up lp in each ch across, turn. (30 lps on hook)

Rows 2–92: Rep rows 2–5 of Capelet consecutively, ending with row 4. (Neck ribbing will form opening of Pouch.) At end of last row, leaving long end for sewing, fasten off.
Matching sts, using single strand of ecru, sew first and last rows tog.
For **bottom,** with 2 strands of gold held tog, weave through ends of gold rows on bottom of Pouch. Pull tight to gather, secure ends.

DRAWSTRING
Make 2.
With size E hook and 1 strand each ecru and gold held tog, ch 120, sl st in 2nd ch from hook and in each ch across. Fasten off.
Starting at seam, weave 1 drawstring through rows 1 inch below opening of Pouch. Knot ends. Starting at opposite side, weave rem drawstring in opposite direction. Knot ends.
Optional: For lining, sew a ¼ inch hem around fabric circle. Hand baste around circle and pull ends to gather to about same size as Pouch. Insert inside Pouch and tack in place just below drawstrings.❑❑

Flower Power

Design by Gayle Bunn for Bernat

SKILL LEVEL
■■□□ EASY

FINISHED SIZE
One size fits most

MATERIALS
- ❏ Bernat Soft Bouclé bulky (chunky) weight yarn (5 oz/255 yds/140g per ball):
  - 2 balls #22425 soft rose
  - 1 ball #06713 white
- ❏ Bernat Boa bulky (chunky) weight eyelash yarn: (1¾ oz/71 yds/50g per ball):
  - 1 ball #81420 love bird
- ❏ Size J/10/6mm crochet hook or size needed to obtain gauge
- ❏ Tapestry needle

GAUGE
3 sts = 1 inch, 3 rows = 2 inches
Take time to check gauge.

INSTRUCTIONS
Rnd 1: With rose, ch 168, sl st in first ch to form ring being careful not to twist ch, ch 3 *(counts as hdc, ch 1)*, sk next ch, [hdc in next ch, ch 1, sk next ch] around, join with sl st in 2nd ch of ch-3. *(84 hdc, 84 ch sps made)*

Rnd 2: Sl st in next ch sp, ch 3, sk all hdc, [hdc in next ch sp, ch 1] around, join.

Next rnds: Rep rnd 2 until piece measures 7 inches from beg.

Next row: For **shaping,** sk all hdc, sl st in next ch sp, ch 3, [hdc in next ch sp, ch 1] 3 times, **hdc dec** *(see Stitch Guide)* in next 2 ch sps, *ch 1, [hdc in next ch sp, ch 1] 4 times, hdc dec in next 2 ch sps, rep from * around, ch 1, join. *(70 ch sps)*

Next rnds: Rep rnd 2 until piece measures 11 inches from beg.

Next rnd: Sl st in next ch sp, ch 3, sk all hdc, [hdc in next ch sp, ch 1] twice, hdc dec in next 2 ch sps, ch 1, *[hdc in next ch sp, ch 1] 3 times, hdc dec in next 2 ch sps, ch 1, rep from * around, join. *(56 ch sps)*

Next rnds: Rep rnd 2 until piece measures 14 inches from beg.

Next rnd: Sl st in next ch sp, ch 3, sk all hdc, hdc in next ch sp, ch 1, [hdc dec in next 2 ch sps, ch 1, hdc in next ch sp, ch 1] around, join. *(38 ch sps)*

Next rnd: Sl st in next ch sp, ch 3, sk all hdc, hdc in next ch sp, ch 1 * hdc dec in next 2 ch sps, ch 1, [hdc in next ch sp, ch 1] twice, rep from * around, join. *(29 ch sps)*

Next rnd: Rep rnd 2.

Next rnd: Sl st in next ch sp, ch 3, sk all hdc, hdc dec in next 2 ch sps, ch 1 *hdc dec in next 2 ch sps, ch 1, [hdc in next ch sp, ch 1] 7 times, rep from * around, join. Fasten off. *(26 hdc, 26 ch sps)*

Next rnd: Join love bird with sc in first st, sc in each ch sp and each st around, join with sl st in first sc.

Next rnd: Ch 1, sc in each st around, join. Fasten off.

BOTTOM EDGING
Rnd 1: With RS facing, working in starting ch on opposite side of row 1, join love bird with sc in first ch, sc in each ch around, join. *(168 sc made)*

Rnd 2: Ch 1, sc in each st around, join. Fasten off.

FLOWER
Rnd 1: With white, ch 2, 5 sc in 2nd ch from hook, join with sl st in first sc. *(5 sc made)*

Rnd 2: Ch 1, 2 sc in each st round, join. *(10 sc)*

Rnd 3: Ch 1, 2 sc in first st, [sc in next st, 2 sc in next st] 4 times, sc in last st, join. *(15 sc)*

Row 4: First petal, ch 1, 2 sc in first st, sc in next st, 2 sc in next st leaving rem sts unworked, turn.

Rows 5–7: Ch 1, sc in each st across, turn.

Row 8: Ch 1, **sc dec** *(see Stitch Guide)* in first 2 sts, sc in next st, sc dec in last 2 sts. Fasten off.

Row 4: 2nd to 5th petals, join white with sl st in next unworked sc on rnd 3, ch 1, 2 sc in same st, sc in next st, 2 sc in next st leaving rem sts unworked, turn.

Rows 5–8: Rep rows 5–8 of first petal. Complete all petals.

Rnd 9: Join love bird with sl st in sp between any 2 petals, ch 1, sc in same sp, evenly sp sc around, join with sl st in first sc. Fasten off.

Center, with love bird, ch 4, [yo, insert hook in 4th ch from hook, yo, pull lp through, yo, pull through 2 lps on hook] 4 times, yo, pull through all lps on hook. Fasten off.

Sew center to center of Flower, sew Flower to top of Poncho as shown in photo.❏❏

Tahitian Dreams

Design by Shelle Cain

SKILL LEVEL
■■□□ EASY

FINISHED SIZE
Small/medium size shown

MATERIALS
❑ Red Heart TLC Macaroon bulky (chunky) weight yarn: 9 oz/345 yds/255g #9316 coconut
❑ Size K/10½/6.5mm crochet hook or size needed to obtain gauge
❑ 17 beads, size and shape of your choice

5 BULKY

GAUGE
2 dc = 1 inch, 1 dc row = 1 inch
Take time to check gauge.

Notes: For larger sizes, use a larger hook and add 1 oz of yarn.
Poncho is worked from neck down.
Thread all beads onto yarn before starting.

SPECIAL STITCH
Bead treble crochet (bead tr): Yo 2 times, insert hook in ch sp, yo, pull lp through, yo, pull through 2 lps on hook, pull up bead, [yo, pull through 2 lps on hook] twice.

INSTRUCTIONS
Rnd 1: Ch 51, sl st in first ch to form ring, being careful not to twist ch (*should slip easily over head*), ch 3 (*counts as first dc*), dc in each ch around, join with sl st in 3rd ch of ch-3. (*51 dc made*)

Rnd 2: Ch 7 (*counts as first tr and ch 3*), tr in same st, sk next 2 sts, [(tr, ch 3, tr) in next st, sk next 2 sts] around, join with sl st in 4th ch of ch-7. (*34 tr, 17 ch sps*)

Rnd 3: Ch 7, tr in same st, sk next st, [(tr, ch 3, tr) in next st, sk next st] around, join.

Rnd 4: Ch 1, sc in first st, ch 5, sk ch sp and next st, [sc in next st, ch 5, sk next ch sp and next st]

around, join with sl st in first sc. (*17 sc, 17 ch sps*)

Rnd 5: Sl st in each of next 3 chs, ch 1, sc in same ch, ch 6, [sc in next ch sp, ch 6] around, join.

Rnd 6: Sl st in each of next 3 chs, ch 1, sc in same ch sp, ch 7, [sc in next ch sp, ch 7] around, join.

Rnd 7: Sl st in each of next 3 chs, ch 4 (*counts as first tr*), (dc, **bead tr** {*see Special Stitch*}, 2 tr) in same ch sp, ch 3, [(2 tr, bead tr, 2 tr) in next ch sp, ch 3] around, join with sl st in 4th ch of ch-4. (*85 tr, 17 ch sps*)

Rnd 8: Ch 1, sc in first st, ch 5, sk next 3 sts, sc in next st, ch 5, [sc in next st, ch 5, sk next 3 sts, sc in next st, ch 5] around, join. (*34 ch sps*)

Rnd 9: Sl st in each of next 3 chs, ch 7, tr in same ch sp, (tr, ch 3, tr)

in each ch sp around, join.

Rnd 10: Ch 1, sc in first st, ch 6, sk next st, [sc in next st, ch 6, sk next st] around, join.

Rnd 11: Sl st in each of next 3 chs, ch 1, sc in same ch sp, ch 7, [sc in next ch sp, ch 7] around, join.

Rnd 12: Sl st in each of next 3 chs, ch 4, 4 tr in same ch sp, ch 3, [5 tr in next ch sp, ch 3] around, join. Fasten off.

FRINGE
Cut 2 strands each 20 inches long. Holding both strands tog, fold in half, insert hook in ch sp indicated, pull fold through ch sp, pull ends through fold. Pull to tighten.
Fringe in every other ch sp around bottom edge.❑❑

Brush Strokes

Design by George Shaheen

SKILL LEVEL
■■□□□ EASY

FINISHED SIZES
Woman's Small/medium (large/extra-large) Instructions are given for smallest size, with larger sizes in parentheses. When only 1 number is given, it applies to all sizes.

MATERIALS
- ❏ Jiffy 100 percent acrylic bulky (chunky) weight yarn from Lion Brand (115 yds/2½ oz per ball): 2 balls country evening #359
- ❏ Size 15 (10mm) knitting needles
- ❏ Size 17 (12.75mm) knitting needles or size needed to obtain gauge
- ❏ Tapestry needle

GAUGE
8 sts = 4 inches/10cm in pat st
To save time, take time to check gauge.

PANEL
Make 2.
With smaller needles, cast on 59 (65) sts.

Row 1 (WS): P1; *k1; p1; rep from * across.

Row 2 (RS): K1; *p1; k1; rep from * across.

Rows 3 and 4: Rep Rows 1 and 2.

Row 5: Rep Row 1.
Change to larger needles.

Row 6: Knit.

Row 7: P1; *yo, p2tog; rep from * across.

Rep Row 7 until piece measures approx 10 (9½) inches, ending with a RS row.
Change to smaller needles.

Next row: Rep Row 7.
Knit one row.

[Rep Rows 1 and 2] twice.
Bind off in pat.

ASSEMBLY
Block pieces to measure 29 x 12 inches (32 x 11½ inches), stretching ribbing slightly to maintain retangular shape of pieces.
Referring to Fig. 1, sew pieces tog.❏❏

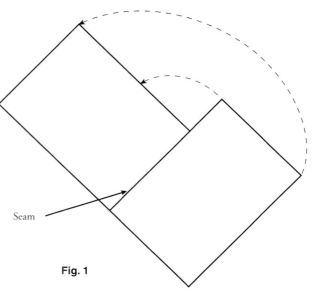

Seam

Fig. 1

Granny Lace

Designs by Lainie Hering

ADULT

SKILL LEVEL
■■□□ EASY

FINISHED SIZE
One size fits most

MATERIALS
- Plymouth Wildflower light (D.K.) weight yarn (2¾ oz/136 yds/50g per ball): 5 balls #47 black
- Plymouth Eros novelty weight nylon ladder yarn (2 oz/165 yds/50g per ball): 2 balls #3017 black
- Size H/8/5mm crochet hook or size needed to obtain gauge
- Tapestry needle
- 2 decorative 1-inch beads

GAUGE
Squares are 8 inches square.
Take time to check gauge.

SPECIAL STITCHES
Beginning popcorn (beg pc): Ch 4 *(counts as first tr)*, 3 tr in sp indicated, drop lp from hook, insert hook in top of beg ch-4, pull dropped lp through.
Popcorn (pc): 4 tr in sp indicated, drop lp from hook, insert hook in first tr of group, pull dropped lp through.

INSTRUCTIONS
SQUARE
Make 6.
Rnd 1: With Wildflower, ch 5, sl st in first ch to form ring, **beg pc** *(see Special Stitches)* in ring, ch 3, [**pc** *(see Special Stitches)* in ring, ch 3] 3 times, join with sl st in 4th ch of beg pc. *(4 pc, 4 ch sps made)*
Rnd 2: (Sl st, ch 4, 2 tr, ch 3, 3 tr) in first ch sp, ch 1, *(3 tr, ch 3, 3 tr) in next ch sp, ch 1, rep from * around, join with sl st in 4th ch of ch-4. *(24 tr, 4 ch-1 sps, 4 ch-3 sps)*
Rnd 3: Sl st in each of next 2 sts, (sl

st, ch 4, 2 tr, ch 3, 3 tr) in next ch-3 sp, ch 2, 3 tr in next ch-1 sp, ch 2, *(3 tr, ch 3, 3 tr) in next ch-3 sp, ch 2, 3 tr in next ch-1 sp, ch 2, rep from * around, join. *(36 tr, 8 ch-2 sps, 4 ch-3 sps)*

Rnds 4–6: Sl st in each of next 2 sts, (sl st, ch 4, 2 tr, ch 3, 3 tr) in next ch-3 sp, ch 2, [3 tr in next ch-2 sp, ch 2] across to next corner ch-3 sp, *(3 tr, ch 3, 3 tr) in next ch-3 sp, ch 2, [3 tr in next ch-2 sp, ch 2] across to next corner ch-3 sp, rep from * around, join. At end of last rnd, fasten off. *(72 tr, 20 ch-2 sps, 4 ch-3 sps)*

With RS tog, sew 3 Squares tog for back and front according to illustration. Sew shoulders as indicated on illustration.

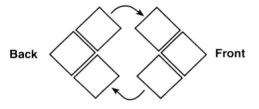

Back   Front

TRIM
Working around bottom edge, join Wildflower with sl st in any tr, ch 3 *(counts as first dc),* dc in each tr and in each sp around with 2 dc in each joining, join with sl st in 3rd ch of ch-3. Fasten off.

Rep around neck edge, working dc 3 sts tog at each V.

DRAWSTRING
With Wildflower, leaving 5-inch end at beg and end, make ch 55 inches in length. Fasten off.

Weave drawstring through sts around neck edge beg and ending in front. Thread one bead on each end. Tie a knot in each end to secure bead. Trim ends close to bead.

FRINGE
Cut one strand Eros, 18 inches long, fold in half, insert hook in st, pull fold through, pull ends through fold. Pull to tighten.

Fringe in every other st around bottom edge.❑❑

SKILL LEVEL
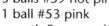 ■■□□□ EASY

FINISHED SIZE
Girls 2–5 [6–10] years

MATERIALS
❑ Plymouth Wildflower light (D.K.) yarn (2¾ oz/136 yds/50g per ball):
   3 balls #59 hot pink
   1 ball #53 pink
❑ Plymouth Eros novelty weight nylon ladder yarn:
   2 oz/165 yds/50g #2010 hot pink
❑ Size H/8/5mm crochet hook or size needed to obtain gauge
❑ Tapestry needle
❑ Decorative beads of choice

GAUGE
Squares are 6 [7] inches square.

SPECIAL STITCHES
Beginning popcorn (beg pc): Ch 3 *(counts as first dc),* 3 dc in sp indicated, drop lp from hook, insert hook in top of beg ch-3, pull dropped lp through.

Popcorn (pc): 4 dc in sp indicated, drop lp from hook, insert hook in first dc of group, pull dropped lp through.

INSTRUCTIONS
SQUARE NO.1
Make 4.

Rnd 1: With pink Wildflower, ch 5, sl st in first ch to form ring, **beg pc** *(see Special Stitches)* in ring, ch 3, [**pc** *(see Special Stitches)* in ring, ch 3] 3 times, join with sl st in 3rd ch of beg pc. Fasten off. *(4 pc, 4 ch sps made)*

Rnd 2: Join hot pink Wildflower with sl st in first ch sp, (ch 3, 2 dc, ch 3, 3 dc) in same ch sp, ch 1, *(3 dc, ch 3, 3 dc) in next ch sp, ch 1, rep from * around, join with sl st in 3rd ch of beg ch-3. *(24 dc, 4 ch-1 sps, 4 ch-3 sps)*

Rnd 3: Sl st in each of next 2 sts, (sl st, ch 3, 2 dc, ch 3, 3 dc) in next ch-3 sp, ch 2, 3 dc in next ch-1 sp, ch 2,

*(3 dc, ch 3, 3 dc) in next ch-3 sp, ch 2, 3 dc in next ch-1 sp, ch 2, rep from * around, join. *(36 dc, 8 ch-2 sps, 4 ch-3 sps)*

Rnds 4–6 [7]: Sl st in each of next 2 sts, (sl st, ch 3, 2 dc, ch 3, 3 dc) in next ch sp, ch 2, [3 dc in next ch-2 sp, ch 2] across to next corner ch-3 sp, *(3 dc, ch 3, 3 dc) in next ch-3 sp, ch 2, [3 dc in next ch-2 sp, ch 2] across to next corner ch-3 sp, rep from * around, join. At end of last rnd, fasten off. *(72 [84] dc, 20 [24] ch-2 sps, 4 [4] ch-3 sps)*

SQUARE NO. 2
Make 2.

Rnd 1: With pink Wildflower, ch 5, sl st in first ch to form ring, beg pc in ring, ch 3, [pc in ring, ch 3] 3 times, join with sl st in 3rd ch of beg pc. *(4 pc, 4 ch sps made)*

Rnd 2: (Sl st, ch 3, 2 dc, ch 3, 3 dc) in first ch sp, ch 1, *(3 dc, ch 3, 3 dc) in next ch sp, ch 1, rep from * around, join with sl st in 3rd ch of beg ch-3. Fasten off. *(24 dc, 4 ch-1 sps, 4 ch-3 sps)*

Rnd 3: Join hot pink Wildflower with sl st in first ch sp, (ch 3, 2 dc, ch 3, 3 dc) in same ch sp, ch 2, 3 dc in next ch-1 sp, ch 2, *(3 dc, ch 3, 3 dc) in next ch-3 sp, ch 2, 3 dc in next ch-1 sp, ch 2, rep from * around, join. *(36 dc, 8 ch-2 sps, 4 ch-3 sps)*

Rnds 4–6 [7]: Sl st in each of next 2 sts, (sl st, ch 3, 2 dc, ch 3, 3 dc) in next ch sp, ch 2, [3 dc in next ch-2 sp, ch 2] across to next corner ch-3 sp, *(3 dc, ch 3, 3 dc) in next ch-3 sp, ch 2, [3 dc in next ch-2 sp, ch 2] across to next corner ch-3 sp, rep from * around, join. At end of last rnd, fasten off. *(72 [84] dc, 20 [24] ch-2 sps, 4 [4] ch-3 sps)*

With RS tog, sew 3 Squares tog for back and front according to illustration. Sew shoulders as indicated on illustration.

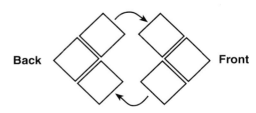

Back   Front

TRIM

Rnd 1: Working around bottom edge, join hot pink Wildflower with sl st in any dc, ch 3 *(counts as first st)*, dc in each dc and in each sp around with 2 dc in each joining, join with sl st in 3rd ch of ch-3.

Rnd 2: Ch 3, dc in each st around with 2 dc in each point, join. Fasten off. Rep around neck edge, working dc 3 sts tog at each V.

DRAWSTRING

With hot pink Wildflower, leaving 5-inch end at beg and end, make ch 43 inches in length. Fasten off.

Weave drawstring through sts around neck edge beg and ending in front. Thread beads on each end. Tie a knot in each end to secure beads. Trim ends close to beads.

FRINGE

Cut 1 strand Eros, 10 inches long, fold in half, insert hook in st, pull fold through, pull ends through fold. Pull to tighten.

Fringe in every other st around bottom edge.❏❏

Cabled Fisherman

Design by Darla Sims

SKILL LEVEL
■■■□ INTERMEDIATE

FINISHED SIZE
One size fits all

MATERIALS
❏ Lion Brand Wool Ease medium (worsted) yarn: 17½ oz/875 yds/496g #99 fisherman **4 MEDIUM**
❏ Size H/8/5mm and I/9/5.5mm crochet hooks or sizes needed to obtain gauge

GAUGE
Size H hook: 7 dc = 2 inches
Size I hook: 3 dc = 1 inch, 3 dc rows = 2 inches
Take time to check gauge.

SPECIAL STITCHES
Front post double crochet (fpdc): Working around post of st (see Stitch Guide), yo, insert hook from front to back and back to front, yo, pull lp through, complete for dc.

Cable: Sk next 2 sts, **fpdc** (see Special Stitches) around each of next 2 sts, working in front of last 2 fpdc, fpdc around each sk st.

Large cable: Sk next 2 sts, fpdc around each of next 2 sts, working in front of last 2 fpdc, fpdc around each sk st, fpdc around each of next 2 sts.

Reverse large cable (rev large cable): Fpdc around each of next 2 sts, sk next 2 sts, fpdc around each of next 2 sts, working in front of last 2 fpdc, fpdc around each sk st.

INSTRUCTIONS
PONCHO
Rnd 1: With size I hook, ch 80, sl st in first ch to form ring, ch 3 (counts as first dc), dc in same ch, dc in each of next 14 chs, 2 dc in next ch, dc in each of next 4 chs, [2 dc in next ch, dc in each of next 14 chs, 2 dc in next ch, dc in each of next 4 chs] around, join with sl st in 3rd ch of beg ch-3. (88 dc made)

Rnd 2: Ch 3, dc in same st, dc in each of next 16 sts, 2 dc in next st, **cable** (see Special Stitches), *2 dc in next st, dc in each of next 16 sts, 2 dc in next st, cable*, 2 dc in next st, dc in each of next 5 sts, **large cable** (see Special Stitches), dc in each of next 5 sts, 2 dc in next st, cable, rep between *, join with sl st in 3rd ch of beg ch-3. (74 dc, 4 cables, 1 large cable)

Rnd 3: Ch 3, dc in same st, [dc in each st across to st before next cable, 2 dc in next st, cable, 2 dc in next st] twice, dc in each st across to next large cable, **rev large cable** (see Special Stitches), dc in each st across to st before next cable, 2 dc in next st, cable, 2 dc in next st, dc in each st across to st before last cable, 2 dc in next st, cable, join with sl st in 3rd ch of beg ch-3.

Rnd 4: Ch 3, dc in same st, [dc in each st across to st before next cable, 2 dc in next st, cable, 2 dc in next st] twice, dc in each st across to next rev large cable, large cable; dc in each st across to st before next cable, 2 dc in next st, cable, 2 dc in next st, dc in each st across to st before last cable, 2 dc in next st, cable, join with sl st in 3rd ch of beg ch-3.

Rnds 5–19: Rep rnds 3 and 4 alternately, ending with rnd 3.

Rnd 20: Ch 3, [dc in each st across to next cable, cable] twice, dc in each st across to next rev large cable, large cable, [dc in each st across to next cable, cable] twice, join with sl st in 3rd ch of beg ch-3.

Rnd 21: Ch 3, [dc in each st across to next cable, cable] twice, dc in each st across to next large cable, rev large cable, [dc in each st across to next cable, cable] twice, join with sl st in 3rd ch of beg ch-3.

Rnds 22–26: Rep rnds 20 and 21 alternately, ending with rnd 20.

Rnd 27: Ch 4 (counts as first dc and next ch-1 sp), sk next st, [dc in next st, ch 1, sk next st] around, join with sl st in 3rd ch of beg ch-4.

Rnd 28: Ch 3, dc in each st and in each ch sp around, join with sl st in 3rd ch of ch-3.

Rnds 29–31: Rep rnds 27 and 28 alternately, ending with rnd 27.

Rnd 32: Sl st in first ch sp, ch 1, (sc, ch 15, sc) in same sp, (sc, ch 15, sc) in each ch sp around, join with sl st in beg sc. Fasten off.

COLLAR
Rnd 1: Working in starting ch on opposite side of rnd 1, with size H hook, join with sl st in first ch, ch 3, dc in each ch around, join with sl st in 3rd ch of beg ch-3. (80 dc made)

Rnd 2: Ch 4 (counts as first dc and next ch-1 sp), sk next st, [dc in next st, ch 1, sk next st] around, join with sl st in 3rd ch of ch-4.

Rnd 3: Ch 3, dc in each st and in each ch sp around, join with sl st in 3rd ch of beg ch-3. Fasten off.❏❏

Posh

Design by George Shaheen

SKILL LEVEL
■■□□ EASY

FINISHED SIZES
Small/medium (large/extra-large) Instructions are given for smallest size, with larger sizes in parentheses. When only 1 number is given, it applies to all sizes.

MATERIALS
- ❏ Divine 79½ percent acrylic/18 percent mohair/2½ percent polyester bulky weight yarn from Patons (142 yds/100g per skein): **5 BULKY**
    - 2 skeins halo blue #06106 (MC)
- ❏ Cha Cha 100 percent nylon novelty eyelash super bulky weight yarn from Patons (77 yds/50g per ball): **6 SUPER BULKY**
    - 2 balls hippie #02007 (CC)
- ❏ Size 13 (9mm) 39-inch circular needle
- ❏ Size 15 (10mm) 39-inch circular needle
- ❏ Size 17 (12.75) 39-inch circular needle or size needed to obtain gauge
- ❏ 1 (1¼ inch) button
- ❏ Sewing needle and matching thread

GAUGE
6½ sts = 4 inches/10cm in pat st with MC and largest needle
To save time, take time to check gauge.

PATTERN NOTES
Circular needle is used to accommodate large number of sts. Do not join; work in rows.

CC is used doubled; 1 strand is used of MC.

Slip all sts knitwise.

When measuring, be sure piece is flat and not stretched, as this pattern tends to grow vertically and shrink horizontally.

PONCHO
With size 17 needle and 2 strands of CC held tog, cast on 87 (99) sts.

Knit 5 rows.

Cut CC, join MC. Knit 1 row.

Rows 1 and 3 (WS): K1, purl to last st, k1.

Row 2: K3, [yo, sl 1, k2tog, psso, yo, k3] 14 (16) times.

Row 4: K1, k2tog, yo, [k3, yo, sl 1, k2tog, psso, yo] 13 (15) times, yo, k3, yo, ssk, k1.

Rep Rows 1 – 4 until piece measures approx 16 (17) inches, ending with a RS row.

Change to size 15 needle.

Rep Rows 1 – 4 until piece measures approx 19 (20) inches, ending with a RS row.

Change to size 13 needle.

Rep Rows 1 – 4 until piece measures approx 22 (23) inches, ending with a WS row.

Next row (WS): Rep Row 1.

Bind off purlwise.

ASSEMBLY
Block piece to measure 52 x 22½ (59 x 23½) inches.

Lay piece with WS facing. Fold RH edge and LH edge to meet at center. Sew upper RH corner over upper LH corner at 45 degree angle, overlapping 2 (2½) inches at neck edge.

Sew button through all layers of closure.❏❏

Butterflies

Design by George Shaheen

SKILL LEVEL

■■□□ EASY

FINISHED SIZES

Woman's small/medium (large/extra-large) Instructions are given for smallest size, with larger sizes in parentheses. When only 1 number is given, it applies to all sizes.

MATERIALS

❏ Divine 79½ percent acrylic/18 percent mohair/2½ percent polyester bulky weight yarn from Patons (142 yds/100g per ball): 5 (6) balls chantilly rose #06406

❏ Size 17 (12.75) 36-inch circular needle or size required for gauge

5 BULKY

GAUGE

11 sts = 6 inches/15 cm in pat st
To save time, take time to check gauge.

PATTERN NOTE

Circular needle is used to accommodate large number of sts. Do not join; work in rows.

PANEL

Make 2.
Cast on 81 (85) sts.
Row 1 (RS): Purl.
Row 2 and all WS rows: Knit.
Row 3: P5 (7), [yo, p2tog, p8] 7 times, yo, p2tog, p4 (6).
Row 5: P3 (5), [p2tog, yo, p1, yo, p2tog, p5] 7 times, p2tog, yo, p1, yo, p2tog, p3 (5).
Row 7: P4 (6), [p2tog, yo, p8] 7 times, p2tog, yo p5 (7).
Row 9: Purl.
Row 11: P10 (12), [yo, p2tog, p8] 7 times, p1 (3).
Row 13: P8 (10), [p2tog, yo, p1, yo, p2tog, p5] 7 times, p3 (5).
Row 15: P9 (11), [p2tog, yo, p8] 7 times, p2 (4).
Row 16: Knit.

Rep Rows 1–16 until panel measures approx 22 (23) inches, ending with a WS row.
Bind off purlwise.

ASSEMBLY

Block panels to measure 44 x 22 inches (46 x 23 inches).
Sew bound-off edges of panels tog for shoulder seams, leaving center 12 (13) inches open for neck.

FRINGE

Cut strands of yarn, each 6 inches long.
Holding 2 strands tog, fold each group in half.
Working along one edge, insert crochet hook from WS to RS. Pull fold of fringe through fabric. Draw ends through loop and fasten tightly.
Tie fringe in every other st along arm edge.
Rep along opposite arm edge.
Trim fringe evenly.❏❏

CROCHET

Blue Roses

Design by Belinda "Bendy" Carter

FINISHED SIZE
One size fits most.

FINISHED GARMENT MEASUREMENT
Length: 22 inches
Neck circumference: 24 inches
Bottom circumference: 72 inches

MATERIALS
❑ Lion Brand Wool-Ease medium (worsted) weight yarn (2.5 oz/ 162 yds/70g per skein):
    7 skeins #301 white glitter (MC)
❑ Lion Brand Fun Fur bulky (chunky) weight eyelash yarn (1.5 oz/ 57 yds/40g per skein):
    6 skeins #203 indigo (CC)
❑ Coats Dual Duty Plus All Purpose Thread Art. No. 210 (300 yds per spool):
    2 spools #4D firmament blue (A)
❑ Sulky Silver Metallic Thread (250 yds per spool):
    1 spool #8040 opalescent (B)
❑ Sizes H/8/5mm and K/10½/ 6.5mm crochet hooks or size needed to obtain gauge
❑ Size 10/1.15mm steel crochet hook
❑ Beading needle
❑ Sewing needle
❑ 49 silver size 4mm faceted beads

GAUGE
Size K hook and MC: 3 sc = 1 inch
Take time to check gauge.

PONCHO
Rnd 1 (RS): With size K hook and MC, beg at neck, ch 72, join with sl st to form ring, ch 1, sc in each ch around, join with sl st in first sc, **turn**. Fasten off. *(72 sc)*
Rnd 2: With WS facing, using size K hook, join 2 strands CC held tog with

a sl st in last sc of last rnd, ch 1, sc in same st as joining and in each rem sc around, join with sl st in first sc, turn. Fasten off.
Rnd 3: With RS facing, using size K hook, join MC with a sl st in last sc of last rnd, ch 1, sc in same sc as joining and in each of next 2 sc, [2 sc in next sc, sc in each of next 2 sc] around, join with sl st in first sc, **do not turn**. *(96 sc)*
Rnd 4: Ch 1, (sc, dc) in same st as joining, sk next st, [(sc, dc) in next st, sk next st] around, do not join or turn.
Rnds 5–8: *Note: Do not join rnds unless otherwise stated. Mark first st of each rnd with safety pin or other small marker.* (Sc, dc) in first sc, sk next dc, [(sc, dc) in next st, sk next dc] around, do not turn.
Rnd 9: 2 sc in first st, sc in each of next 3 sts, [2 sc in next st, sc in each of next 3 sts] around, join with sl st in first sc, turn. Fasten off. *(120 sc)*
Rnd 10: Rep rnd 2.
Rnd 11: With RS facing, join MC with a sl st in first sc, ch 1, 2 sc in same st, sc in each of next 4 sc, [2 sc in next sc, sc in each of next 4 sc] around, join with sl st in first sc, do not turn. *(144 sc)*
Rnds 12–16: Rep rnds 4–8.
Rnd 17: 2 sc in first st, sc in each of next 5 sts, [2 sc in next st, sc in each of next 5 sts] around, join with sl st in first sc, turn. Fasten off. *(168 sc)*
Rnd 18: Rep rnd 2.
Rnd 19: With RS facing, join MC with a sl st in first sc, ch 1, 2 sc in same st, sc in each of next 6 sc, [2 sc in next sc, sc in each of next 6 sc] around, join with sl st in first sc, do not turn. *(192 sc)*
Rnds 20–24: Rep rnds 4–8.
Rnd 25: 2 sc in first st, sc in each of next 7 sts, [2 sc in next st, sc in each of next 7 sts] around, join with sl st in first sc, turn. Fasten off. *(216 sc)*
Rnd 26: Rep rnd 2.
Rnd 27: With RS facing, join MC with a sl st in first sc, ch 1, sc in same sc, sc in each rem sc around, join with sl st in first sc.
Rnds 28–32: Rep rnds 4–8.

Rnd 33: Sc in each st around, join with sl st in first sc, turn. Fasten off.
Rnd 34: Rep rnd 2.
Rnds 35–58: Rep rnds 27–34 consecutively 3 times.

NECK EDGING
Rnd 1: With size H hook, RS facing, working in rem lps of foundation ch at base of rnd 1 of Poncho, join MC with a sl st in first rem lp, ch 2 (counts as first hdc throughout), hdc in each rem st around, join with sl st in 2nd ch of beg ch-2, do not turn. *(72 hdc)*
Rnd 2: Ch 2, [**fpdc** (see Stitch Guide) over next hdc, **bpdc** (see Stitch Guide) over next hdc] around to last hdc, fpdc over last hdc, join with sl st in 2nd ch of beg ch-2, do not turn.
Rnd 3: Ch 1, sc in same st as joining, ch 3, **fpsc** (see Stitch Guide) over next st, ch 3, [**bpsc** (see Stitch Guide) over next st, ch 3, fpsc over next st, ch 3] around, join with sl st in beg sc. Fasten off.

FLOWER
Make 7.
Rnd 1: With size 10 hook, holding 2 strands A and 1 strand B tog, ch 6, join with sl st to form a ring, ch 6 (counts as first dc, ch-3), dc in ring, [ch 3, dc in ring] 6 times, ch 3, join with sl st in 3rd ch of beg ch-6. *(8 ch-3 sps)*
Rnd 2: (Sl st, ch 1, sc, 4 dc, sc, sl st) in each ch-3 sp around, do not join. *(8 petals)*
Rnd 3: Working behind petals of last rnd, [ch 4, sl st between next 2 petals] around. *(8 ch-4 sps)*
Rnd 4: (Sl st, ch 1, sc, 6 dc, sc, sl st) in each ch-4 sp around, do not join. *(8 petals)*
Rnd 5: Working behind petals of last rnd, [ch 5, sl st between next 2 petals] around. *(8 ch-5 sps)*
Rnd 6: (Sl st, ch 1, sc, 8 dc, sc, sl st) in each ch-5 sp around, join with sl st in beg sl st. Fasten off.
With beading needle, sew 7 beads to center of each Flower. With sewing needle and A, sew 1 flower to each MC section down center front of Poncho.❑❑

Lacy Fans

Design by Mary Layfield

SKILL LEVEL
■■■□ INTERMEDIATE

FINISHED SIZE
One size fits most

MATERIALS
❑ Caron Simply Soft medium (worsted) weight yarn:
    24 oz/1,000 yds/570g #9719 soft pink
❑ Size G/6/4mm crochet hook or size needed to obtain gauge
❑ Tapestry needle

GAUGE
4 dc = 1 inch, 2 dc rows = 1 inch
Take time to check gauge.

SPECIAL STITCH
Cluster (cl): Yo, insert hook in st, yo, pull lp through st, yo, pull through 2 lps on hook, [yo, insert hook in same st, yo, pull lp through st, yo, pull through 2 lps on hook] 3 times, yo, pull through all lps on hook.

INSTRUCTIONS
LEFT SIDE
Row 1: Ch 72, sc in 2nd ch from hook and in each ch across, turn. *(71 sc made)*

Row 2: Ch 3 *(counts as first dc)*, dc in each st across, turn.

Row 3: Ch 3, [dc in each of next 5 dc, ch 6, sk next 4 sts, sc in next st, ch 3, sk next st, sc in next st, ch 6, sk next 4 sts] across to last 6 sts, dc in each of last 6 dc, turn. *(27 dc, 8 sc, 8 ch-6 sps, 4 ch-3 sps)*

Row 4: Ch 3, [dc in each of next 5 dc, ch 3, sc in next ch-6 sp, ch 1, 7 dc in next ch-3 sp, ch 1, sc in next ch-6 sp, ch 2] across to last 6 sts, dc in each of last 6 sts, turn. *(55 dc, 8 sc)*

Row 5: Ch 3, dc in each of next 5 sts, *ch 1, sk next sc, [cl *(see Special Stitch)* in next st, ch 3, sk next st] 3 times, cl in next st, ch 1, sk next sc, dc in each of next 5 sts, rep from * across, dc in last st, turn. *(27 dc, 16 cls, 12 ch-3 sps)*

Row 6: Ch 3, *dc in each of next 5 dc, ch 2, [sc in next ch-3 sp, ch 3] twice, sc in next ch-3 sp, ch 2, rep from * 3 times, dc in each of last 6 dc turn. *(27 dc, 8 ch-3 sps)*

Row 7: Ch 3, [dc in each of next 5 dc, ch 4, sc in next ch-3 sp, ch 3, sc in next ch-3 sp, ch 4] 4 times, dc in each of last 6 dc, turn. *(27 dc, 8 ch-4 sps, 4 ch-3 sps)*

Row 8: Ch 3, [dc in each of next 5 dc, ch 3, sc in next ch-4 sp, ch 1, 7 dc in next ch-3 sp, ch 1, sc in next ch-4 sp, ch 2] across to last 6 sts, dc in each of last 6 dc, turn. *(55 dc, 8 sc)*

Rows 9–12: Rep rows 5–8.

Rows 13 & 14: Rep rows 5 and 6.

Row 15: For **shoulder shaping,** ch 1, sc in each of first 4 sts, hdc in next st, dc in next st, [ch 4, sc in next ch-3 sp, ch 3, sc in next ch-3 sp, ch 4, dc in each of next 5 dc] 4 times, dc in last st, turn. *(22 dc, 12 sc, 1 hdc, 8 ch-4 sps, 4 ch-3 sps)*

Row 16: Ch 3, [dc in each of next 5 dc, ch 3, sc in next ch-4 sp, ch 1, 7 dc in next ch-3 sp, ch 1, sc in next ch-4 sp, ch 2] across to last 6 sts, dc in next st, hdc in next st, sc in each of last 4 sts, turn. *(50 dc, 12 sc, 1 hdc)*

Row 17: Ch 1, sc in each of first 4 sts, hdc in next st, dc in next st, *ch 1, sk next sc, [cl in next st, ch 3, sk next st] 3 times, cl in next st, ch 1, sk next st, dc in each of next 5 dc, rep from * across, dc in last dc, turn. *(22 dc, 4 sc, 1 hdc, 16 cls, 12 ch-3 sps)*

Row 18: Ch 3, *dc in each of next 5 dc, ch 2, [sc in next ch-3 sp, ch 3] twice, sc in next ch-3 sp, ch 2, rep from * 3 times, dc in next st, hdc in next st, sc in each of last 4 sts, turn. *(22 dc, 16 sc, 1 hdc, 8 ch-3 sps)*

Row 19: Ch 1, sc in each of first 4 sts, hdc in next st, dc in next st, [ch 4, sc in next ch-3 sp, ch 3, sc in next ch-3 sp, ch 4, dc in each of next 5 dc] 4 times, dc in last st, turn. *(22 dc, 12 sc, 1 hdc, 8 ch-4 sps, 4 ch-3 sps)*

Row 20: Ch 3, [dc in each of next 5 dc, ch 3, sc in next ch-4 sp, ch 1, 7 dc in next ch-3 sp, ch 1, sc in next ch-4 sp, ch 2] across to last 6 sts, dc in each of next 4 sts, hdc in next st, sc in last st, turn. *(53 dc, 9 sc, 1 hdc, 8 ch-1 sps, 4 ch-2 sps)*

Row 21: Ch 1, sc in each of first 4 sts, hdc in next st, dc in next st *ch 1, sk next sc, [cl in next st, ch 3, sk next st] 3 times, cl in next st, ch 1, sk next st, dc in each of next 5 dc, rep from * across, dc in last dc, turn. *(22 dc, 4 sc, 1 hdc, 16 cls, 12 ch-3 sps)*

Row 22: Ch 3, *dc in each of next 5 dc, ch 2, [sc in next ch-3 sp, ch 3] twice, sc in next ch-3 sp, ch 2 rep from * 3 times, dc in next st, hdc in next st, sc in each of last 4 sts, turn. *(22 dc, 16 sc, 1 hdc, 8 ch-3 sps)*

Row 23: Ch 1, sc in each of first 4 sts, hdc in next st, dc in next st, [ch 4, sc in next ch-3 sp, ch 3, sc in next ch-3 sp, ch 4, dc in each of next 5 dc] 4 times, dc in last st, turn. *(22 dc, 12 sc, 1 hdc, 8 ch-4 sps, 4 ch-3 sps)*

Row 24: Ch 3, [dc in each of next 5 dc, ch 3, sc in next ch-4 sp, ch 1, 7 dc in next ch-3 sp, ch 1, sc in next ch-4 sp, ch 2] across to last 6 sts, dc in each of next 4 sts, hdc in next st, sc in last st, turn. *(53 dc, 9 sc, 1 hdc, 8 ch-1 sps, 4 ch-2 sps)*

Row 25: Ch 1, sc in each of first 4 sts, hdc in next st, dc in next st, *ch 1, sk next sc, [cl in next st, ch 3, sk next st] 3 times, cl in next st, ch 1, sk next st, dc in each of next 5 dc, rep from * across, dc in last dc, turn. *(22 dc, 4 sc, 1 hdc, 16 cls, 12 ch-3 sps)*

Row 26: Ch 3, *dc in each of next 5 dc, ch 2, [sc in next ch-3 sp, ch 3] twice, sc in next ch-3 sp, ch 2, rep from * 3 times, dc in next st, hdc in next st, sc in each of last 4 sts, turn. *(22 dc, 16 sc, 1 hdc, 8 ch-3 sps)*

Row 27: Ch 1, sc in each of first 4 sts, hdc in next st, dc in next st, [ch 4, sc in next ch-3 sp, ch 3, sc in next ch-3 sp, ch 4, dc in each of next 5 dc] 4 times, dc in last st, turn. *(22 dc, 12 sc, 1 hdc, 8 ch-4 sps, 4 ch-3 sps)*

Row 28: Ch 3, [dc in each of next 5 dc, ch 3, sc in next ch-4 sp, ch 1, 7 dc in next ch-3 sp, ch 1, sc in next ch-4 sp, ch 2] across to last 6 sts, dc in each of next 4 sts, hdc in next st, sc in last st, turn. *(50 dc, 12 sc, 1 hdc, 8 ch-1 sps, 8 ch-3 sps)*

Rows 29–72: Rep rows 5–8 consecutively. At end of last row, fasten off.

RIGHT SIDE

Row 1: Ch 72, sc in 2nd ch from hook and in each ch across, turn. *(71 sc made)*

Row 2: Ch 3 *(counts as first dc)*, dc in each st across, turn.

Row 3: Ch 3, [dc in each of next 5 dc, ch 6, sk next 4 sts, sc in next st, ch 3, sk next st, sc in next st, ch 6, sk next 4 sts] across to last 6 sts, dc in each of last 6 dc, turn. *(27 dc, 8 sc, 8 ch-6 sps, 4 ch-3 sps)*

Row 4: Ch 3, [dc in each of next 5 dc, ch 3, sc in next ch-6 sp, ch 1, 7 dc in next ch-3 sp, ch 1, sc in next ch-6 sp, ch 2] across to last 6 sts, dc in each of last 6 dc, turn. *(55 dc)*

Row 5: Ch 3, dc in each of next 5 sts, *ch 1, sk next sc, [cl in next st, ch 3, sk next st] 3 times, cl in next st, ch 1, sk next st, dc in each of next 5 sts, rep from * across, dc in last st, turn. *(27 dc, 16 cls, 12 ch-3 sps)*

Row 6: Ch 3, *dc in each of next 5 dc, ch 2, [sc in next ch-3 sp, ch 3] twice, sc in next ch-3 sp, ch 2, rep from * 3 times, dc in each of last 6 dc, turn. *(27 dc, 8 ch-3 sps)*

Row 7: Ch 3, [dc in each of next 5 dc, ch 4, sc in next ch-3 sp, ch 3, sc in next ch-3 sp, ch 4] 4 times, dc in each of last 6 dc, turn. *(27 dc, 8 ch-4 sps, 4 ch-3 sps)*

Row 8: Ch 3, [dc in each of next 5 dc, ch 3, sc in next ch-4 sp, ch 1, 7 dc in next ch-3 sp, ch 1, sc in next ch-4 sp, ch 2] across to last 6 sts, dc in each of last 6 dc, turn. *(55 dc)*

Rows 9–44: Rep rows 5–8 consecutively.

Row 45: Rep row 5.

Row 46: For **shoulder shaping**, ch 3, *dc in each of next 5 dc, ch 2, [sc in next ch-3 sp, ch 3] twice, sc in next ch-3 sp, ch 2, rep from * 3 times, dc in next st, hdc in next st, sc in each of last 4 sts, turn. *(22 dc, 16 sc, 1 hdc, 8 ch-3 sps)*

Row 47: Ch 1, sc in each of first 4 sts, hdc in next st, dc in next st, [ch 4, sc

in next ch-3 sp, ch 3, sc in next ch-3 sp, ch 4, dc in each of next 5 dc] 4 times, dc in last dc, turn. *(22 dc, 12 sc, 1 hdc, 8 ch-4 sps, 4 ch-3 sps)*

Row 48: Ch 3, [dc in each of next 5 dc, ch 3, sc in next ch-4 sp, ch 1, 7 dc in next ch-3 sp, ch 1, sc in next ch-4 sp, ch 2] across to last 6 sts, dc in next st, hdc in next st, sc in each of last 4 sts, turn. *(50 dc, 12 sc, 1 hdc)*

Row 49: Ch 1, sc in each of first 4 sts, hdc in next st, dc in next st, *ch 1, sk next sc, [cl in next st, ch 3, sk next st] 3 times, cl in next st, ch 1, sk next st, dc in each of next 5 sts, rep from * across, dc in last st, turn. *(22 dc, 4 sc, 1 hdc, 16 cls, 12 ch-3 sps)*

Row 50: Ch 3, *dc in each of next 5 dc, ch 2, [sc in next ch-3 sp, ch 3] twice, sc in next ch-3 sp, ch 2, rep from * 3 times, dc in each of next 4 sts, hdc in next st, sc in last st, turn. *(25 dc, 13 sc, 1 hdc, 8 ch-3 sps)*

Row 51: Ch 1, sc in each of first 4 sts, hdc in next st, dc in next st, [ch 4, sc in next ch-3 sp, ch 3, sc in next ch-3 sp, ch 4, dc in each of next 5 dc] 4 times, dc in last dc, turn. *(22 dc, 12 sc, 1 hdc, 8 ch-4 sps, 4 ch-3 sps)*

Row 52: Ch 3, [dc in each of next 5 dc, ch 3, sc in next ch-4 sp, ch 1, 7 dc in next ch-3 sp, ch 1, sc in next ch-4 sp, ch 2] across to last 6 sts, dc in next st, hdc in next st, sc in each of last 4 sts, turn. *(50 dc, 12 sc, 1 hdc)*

Row 53: Ch 1, sc in each of first 4 sts, hdc in next st, dc in next st, *ch 1, sk next sc, [cl in next st, ch 3, sk next st] 3 times, cl in next st, ch 1, sk next st, dc in each of next 5 sts, rep from * across, dc in last st, turn. *(22 dc, 4 sc, 1 hdc, 16 cls, 12 ch-3 sps)*

Row 54: Ch 3, *dc in each of next 5 dc, ch 2, [sc in next ch-3 sp, ch 3] twice, sc in next ch-3 sp, ch 2, rep from * 3 times, dc in each of next 4 sts, hdc in next st, sc in last st, turn. *(25 dc, 13 sc, 1 hdc, 8 ch-3 sps)*

Row 55: Ch 1, sc in each of first 4 sts, hdc in next st, dc in next st, [ch 4, sc in next ch-3 sp, ch 3, sc in next ch-3 sp, ch 4, dc in each of next 5 dc] 4 times, dc in last dc, turn. *(22 dc, 12 sc, 1 hdc, 8 ch-4 sps, 4 ch-3 sps)*

Row 56: Ch 3, [dc in each of next 5 dc, ch 3, sc in next ch-4 sp, ch 1, 7 dc in next ch-3 sp, ch 1, sc in next ch-4 sp, ch 2] across to last 6 sts, dc in next st, hdc in next st, sc in each of last 4 sts, turn. *(50 dc, 12 sc, 1 hdc)*

Row 57: Ch 1, sc in each of first 4 sts, hdc in next st, dc in next st, *ch 1, sk next sc, [cl in next st, ch 3, sk next st] 3 times, cl in next st, ch 1, sk next st, dc in each of next 5 sts, rep from * across, dc in last st, turn. *(22 dc, 4 sc, 1 hdc, 16 cls, 12 ch-3 sps)*

Row 58: Ch 3, *dc in each of next 5 dc, ch 2, [sc in next ch-3 sp, ch 3] twice, sc in next ch-3 sp, ch 2, rep from * 3 times, dc in next st, hdc in next st, sc in each of last 4 sts, turn. *(22 dc, 16 sc, 1 hdc, 8 ch-3 sps)*

Row 59: Ch 1, sc in each of first 4 sts, hdc in next st, dc in next st, [ch 4, sc in next ch-3 sp, ch 3, sc in next ch-3 sp, ch 4, dc in each of next 5 dc] 4 times, dc in last dc, turn. *(22 dc, 12 sc, 1 hdc, 8 ch-4 sps, 4 ch-3 sps)*

Rows 60: Rep row 8.

Rows 61–72: Rep rows 5–8. At end of last row, fasten off.

Sew or crochet pieces tog according to illustration.

NECK TRIM

Join with sc in back seam, dc in next row, evenly space (sc, dc) around, join with sl st in first sc. Fasten off.

TASSEL

Cut 15 pieces of yarn each 10 inches long. Holding 14 pieces tog, tie rem piece around center of pieces, fold in center, using ends of center tie, wrap several times around all pieces ½ inch below fold. Hide ends inside tassel. Sew to center front as shown in photo.

FRINGE

Cut 6 pieces of yarn each 10 inches in length. Holding all 6 pieces tog, fold in half, insert hook in st or row, pull fold through, pull ends through fold. Pull tight.

Fringe in every other dc row or on every 4th st around bottom edge. Trim ends.❏❏

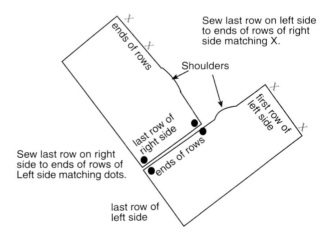

Sew last row on left side to ends of rows of right side matching X.

Shoulders

Sew last row on right side to ends of rows of Left side matching dots.

Zebra Fur

Design by Kathleen Sams for Coats & Clark

SKILL LEVEL
■■□□ EASY

FINISHED SIZE
One size fits most

MATERIALS
- ❑ Red Heart Casual Cot'n Blend bulky (chunky) weight yarn (4 oz/140 yds/113g per skein): 3 skeins #3550 zebra
- ❑ Moda Dea "Jai Alai" bulky (chunky) weight eyelash yarn (1¾ oz/98 yds/59g per ball): 2 balls #6975 gem
- ❑ Size P/15/10mm crochet hook or size needed to obtain gauge
- ❑ Tapestry needle

GAUGE
With 2 strands zebra held tog, 3 dc = 1½ inches; 1 dc row = 1 inch
Take time to check gauge.

PATTERN NOTE
Hold 2 strands of yarn together throughout.

INSTRUCTIONS

SIDE
Make 2.
Row 1 (RS): With 1 strand of each color held tog, ch 29, dc in 4th ch from hook *(first 3 chs count as first dc)* and in each of next 11 chs, 3 dc in next ch, dc in each ch across, turn. *(29 dc made)*

Row 2: Ch 3 *(counts as first dc)*, dc in same st, dc in each of next 13 sts, 3 dc in next st *(center sts)*, dc in each of next 13 sts, 3 dc in last st, turn. *(34 dc)*

Rows 3–8: Ch 3, dc in same st, dc in each st across to 3 center sts, dc in next st, 3 dc in next st, dc in each st across with 2 dc in last st, turn. At end of last row, fasten off gem. *(58 dc)*

Row 9: With 2 strands zebra, ch 3, dc in same st, dc in each of next 27 sts,

3 dc in next st, dc in each st across with 2 dc in last st, turn. *(62 dc)*

Rows 10–13: Ch 3, dc in same st, dc in each st across to 3 center sts, dc in next st, 3 dc in next st, dc in each st across with 2 dc in last st, turn. At end of last row, fasten off 1 strand of zebra. *(78 dc)*

Row 14: With 1 strand of each color held tog, ch 1, sc in each st across to 3 center sts, sc in next st, 3 sc in next st, sc in each st across with 2 sc in last st, turn. *(81 sc)*

Row 15: Ch 1, sc in each st across. Fasten off.
Sew ends of rows on Side pieces tog.

NECK EDGING
With 1 strand of each color held tog, join with sc in any seam, sc evenly spaced around, join with sl st in first sc. Fasten off.❑❑

Goodbye Goosebumps

Design by Kathleen Wesley

FINISHED SIZES

Child's 6 (8, 10, Adult uni-size) Instructions are given for smallest size, with larger sizes in parentheses. When only 1 number is given, it applies to all sizes.

MATERIALS

- TLC® Macaroon™ 100 percent polyester super bulky weight yarn from Coats and Clark (115 yds/85g per ball):
  - 2 (2, 3) balls seaspray #9381 for child's poncho
  - 3 balls pink violet #9351 for adult's poncho
- Size 11 (8mm) needles or size needed to obtain gauge

GAUGE

Child's poncho: 9 sts = 4 inches/10cm in garter st

Adult poncho: 10 sts = 4 inches/10cm in garter st

To save time, take time to check gauge.

SPECIAL ABBREVATION

Kw2: Knit next stitch, wrapping yarn twice around needle.

PATTERN NOTE

Poncho is worked in 2 rectangular pieces then sewn together.

BACK

Cast on 38 (44, 50, 62) sts.

Row 1 (RS): Knit.

Rows 2 – 4: Knit.

Row 5: K1, *Kw2; rep from * to last st, k1.

Row 6: K1, *knit, dropping extra wrap; rep from * to last st, k1.

Rows 7 and 8: Knit.

[Rep Rows 5–8] 4 (5, 7, 10) times.

Next row: Knit.

Bind off loosely knitwise.

FRONT

Work as for back.

ASSEMBLY

Referring to figure, block pieces to measure 7 x 17 (8 x 20, 10 x 22, 14 x 28) inches.

Sew pieces tog as indicated.❏❏

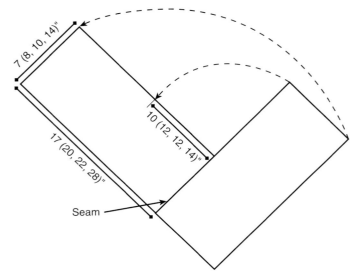

Goodbye Goosebumps

Beaded Aran

Design by Belinda "Bendy" Carter

SKILL LEVEL

■■■□ INTERMEDIATE

FINISHED SIZE
One size fits most

MATERIALS
- ❑ Lion Brand Wool-Ease medium (worsted) weight yarn (3 oz/197 yds/85g per skein): 7 skeins #147 purple
- ❑ Size J/10/6mm crochet hook or size needed to obtain gauge
- ❑ Tapestry needle
- ❑ 500 white 6mm pearl beads

GAUGE
Each Square with Border is 10 inches square.
Take time to check gauge.

SPECIAL STITCHES
Front post double treble left (fpdtr-L): Yo 3 times, insert hook around post *(see Stitch Guide)* of st 2 rows below and 2 sts to the left, yo, pull lp through st, [yo, pull through 2 lps on hook] 4 times, sk st behind post st.

Front post double treble right (fpdtr-R): Yo 3 times, insert hook around post *(see Stitch Guide)* of st 2 rows below and 2 sts to the right, yo, pull lp through st, [yo, pull through 2 lps on hook] 4 times, sk st behind post st.

Front post double treble cross over stitch (fpdtr-ROL): Work fpdtr-L, sc in next st, fpdtr-R over fpdtr-L just made.

Front post double treble cross under stitch (fpdtr-RUL): Work fpdtr-L, sc in next st, fpdtr-R behind last fpdtr-L just made.

Front post treble (fptr): Yo 2 times, insert hook around post of st 2 rows below, yo, pull lp through, [yo, pull through 2 lps on hook] 3 times, sk st behind post st just made.

Pearl: Pull up pearl, sc in next st, all pearl sts are worked on the WS; pearl appears on RS of work.

INSTRUCTIONS
SQUARE NO. 1
Make 2.
Note: Thread 15 pearls onto yarn before beg.
Row 1 (RS): Ch 26, sc in 2nd ch from hook and in each ch across, turn. *(25 sc made)*
Row 2: Ch 1, sc in each st across, turn.
Row 3: Ch 1, sc in first st, [**fpdtr-ROL** *(see Special Stitches),* sc in each of next 2 sts] 4 times, fpdtr-ROL, sc in last st, turn.
Row 4: Ch 1, sc in each of first 2 sts, [**pearl** *(see Special Stitches),* sc in each of next 9 sts] twice, pearl, sc in each of last 2 sts, turn.
Row 5: Ch 1, sc in first st, [**fptr** *(see Special Stitches),* sc in next st, fptr, sc in each of next 7 sts] twice, [fptr, sc in next st] twice, turn.
Rows 6 & 7: Rep rows 2 and 3.
Row 8: Ch 1, sc in each of first 7 sts, pearl, sc in each of next 9 sts, pearl, sc in each of last 7 sts, turn.
Row 9: Ch 1, sc in each of first 6 sts, fptr, sc in next st, fptr, sc in each of next 7 sts, fptr, sc in next st, fptr, sc in each of last 6 sts, turn.
Rows 10–25: Rep rows 2–9 consecutively.
Rows 26 & 27: Rep rows 2 and 3.
Rnd 28: Now working in rnds, ch 1, 3 sc in first st, sc in each st across with 3 sc in last st, working in ends of rows, evenly sp 23 sc across, working in starting ch on opposite side of row 1, 3 sc in first ch, sc in each ch across with 3 sc in last ch, evenly sp 23 sc across ends of rows, join with sl st in first sc. Fasten off. *(104 sc)*

SQUARE NO. 2
Make 2.
Note: Thread 42 pearls onto yarn before beg.
Row 1 (RS): Ch 26, sc in 2nd ch from hook and in each ch across, turn. *(25 sc made)*
Row 2: Ch 1, sc in each st across, turn.
Row 3: Ch 1, sc in each of first 3 sts, [fptr, sc in each of next 5 sts] 3 times, fptr, sc in each of last 3 sts, turn.
Row 4: Ch 1, sc in each of first 3 sts, [pearl, sc in each of next 5 sts] 3 times, pearl, sc in each of last 3 sts, turn.
Row 5: Ch 1, sc in each of first 6 sts, [fptr, sc in each of next 5 sts] twice, fptr, sc in each of last 6 sts, turn.
Row 6: Ch 1, sc in each of first 6 sts, [pearl, sc in each of next 5 sts] twice, pearl, sc in each of last 6 sts, turn.
Rows 7–26: Rep rows 3–6 consecutively.
Row 27: Rep row 3.
Rnd 28: Now working in rnds, ch 1, 3 sc in first st, sc in each st across with 3 sc in last st, working in ends of rows, evenly sp 23 sc across, working in starting ch on opposite side of row 1, 3 sc in first ch, sc in each ch across with 3 sc in last ch, evenly sp 23 sc across ends of rows, join with sl st in first sc. Fasten off. *(104 sc)*

SQUARE NO. 3
Make 2.
Note: Thread 33 pearls onto yarn before beg.
Row 1 (RS): Ch 26, sc in 2nd ch from hook and in each ch across, turn. *(25 sc made)*
Row 2: Ch 1, sc in each st across, turn
Row 3: Ch 1, sc in first st, [**fpdtr-L** *(see Special Stitches),* sc in each of next 3 sts] across, turn.
Row 4: Ch 1, sc in each of first 3 sts, pearl, [sc in each of next 3 sts, pearl] 5 times, sc in last st, turn.
Rows 5 & 6: Ch 1, sc in each st across, turn.
Row 7: Ch 1, sc in each of first 3 sts, fpdtr-L, [sc in each of next 3 sts, fpdtr-L] 4 times, sc in each of last 5 sts, turn.
Row 8: Ch 1, sc in each of first 5 sts, [pearl, sc in each of next 3 sts] 4 times, pearl, sc in each of last 3 sts, turn.
Rows 9 & 10: Ch 1, sc in each st across, turn.

Rows 11–26: Rep rows 3–10 consecutively.

Row 27: Rep row 3.

Rnd 28: Now working in rnds, ch 1, 3 sc in first st, sc in each st across with 3 sc in last st, working in ends of rows, evenly sp 23 sc across, working in starting ch on opposite side of row 1, 3 sc in first ch, sc in each ch across with 3 sc in last ch, evenly sp 23 sc across ends of rows, join with sl st in first sc. Fasten off. *(104 sc)*

SQUARE NO. 4
Make 2.

Note: *Thread 15 pearls onto yarn before beg.*

Row 1 (RS): Ch 26, sc in 2nd ch from hook and in each ch across, turn. *(25 sc made)*

Row 2: Ch 1, sc in each st across, turn.

Row 3: Ch 1, sc in each of first 3 sts, [**fpdtr-R** *(see Special Stitches),* sc in next st, fpdtr-L, sc in each of next 5 sts] twice, fpdtr-R, sc in next st, fpdtr-L, sc in each of last 3 sts, turn.

Row 4: Ch 1, sc in each of first 8 sts, pearl, sc in each of next 7 sts, pearl, sc in each of last 8 sts, turn.

Row 5: Ch 1, sc in each of first 3 sts, [fpdtr-ROL, sc in each of next 5 sts] twice, fpdtr-ROL, sc in each of last 3 sts, turn.

Row 6: Ch 1, sc in each st across, turn.

Row 7: Ch 1, sc in first st, [fpdtr-L, sc in each of next 5 sts, fpdtr-R, sc in next st] across, turn.

Row 8: Ch 1, sc in each of first 4 sts, [pearl, sc in each of next 7 sts] twice, pearl, sc in each of last 4 sts, turn.

Row 9: Ch 1, sc in first st, fptr, [sc in each of next 5 sts, **fpdtr-RUL** *(see Special Stitches)*] twice, sc in each of next 5 sts, fptr, sc in last st, turn.

Row 10: Ch 1, sc in each st across, turn.

Rows 11–26: Rep rows 3–10 consecutively.

Row 27: Rep row 3.

Rnd 28: Now working in rnds, ch 1, 3 sc in first st, sc in each st across with 3 sc in last st, working in ends of rows, evenly sp 23 sc across, working in starting ch on opposite side of row 1, 3 sc in first ch, sc in each ch across

with 3 sc in last ch, evenly sp 23 sc across ends of rows, join with sl st in first sc. Fasten off. *(104 sc)*

SQUARE NO. 5
Make 2.
Note: *Thread 15 pearls onto yarn before beg.*

Row 1 (RS): Ch 26, sc in 2nd ch from hook and in each ch across, turn. *(25 sc made)*

Row 2: Ch 1, sc in each st across, turn

Row 3: Ch 1, sc in each of first 3 sts, [fpdtr-R, sc in next st, fpdtr-L, sc in each of next 5 sts] twice, fpdtr-R, sc in next st, fpdtr-L, sc in each of last 3 sts, turn.

Row 4: Ch 1, sc in each of first 4 sts, [pearl, sc in each of next 7 sts] twice, pearl, sc in each of last 4 sts, turn.

Rows 5 & 6: Ch 1, sc in each st across, turn.

Row 7: Ch 1, sc in first st, [fpdtr-L, sc in each of next 5 sts, fpdtr-R, sc in next st] across, turn.

Row 8: Ch 1, sc in each of first 8 sts, pearl, sc in each of next 7 sts, pearl, sc in each of last 8 sts, turn.

Rows 9 & 10: Ch 1, sc in each st across, turn.

Rows 11–26: Rep rows 3–10 consecutively.

Row 27: Rep row 3.

Rnd 28: Now working in rnds, ch 1, 3 sc in first st, sc in each st across with 3 sc in last st, working in ends of rows, evenly sp 23 sc across, working in starting ch on opposite side of row 1, 3 sc in first ch, sc in each ch across with 3 sc in last ch, evenly sp 23 sc across ends of rows, join with sl st in first sc. Fasten off. *(104 sc)*

SQUARE NO. 6
Make 2.
Note: *Thread 24 pearls onto yarn before beg.*

Row 1 (RS): Ch 26, sc in 2nd ch from hook and in each ch across, turn. *(25 sc made)*

Row 2: Ch 1, sc in each st across, turn.

Row 3: Ch 1, sc in each of first 2 sts, [fpdtr-ROL, sc in each of next 3 sts] 3 times, fpdtr-ROL, sc in each of last 2 sts, turn.

Row 4: Ch 1, sc in each of first 3 sts, [pearl, sc in each of next 5 sts] 3 times, pearl, sc in each of last 3 sts, turn.

Row 5: Ch 1, sc in each of first 2 sts, [fptr, sc in next st, fptr, sc in each of next 3 sts] 3 times, fptr, sc in next st, fptr, sc in each of last 2 sts, turn.

Row 6: Ch 1, sc in each st across, turn.

Rows 7–26: Rep rows 3–6 consecutively.

Row 27: Rep row 3.

Rnd 28: Now working in rnds, ch 1, 3 sc in first st, sc in each st across with 3 sc in last st, working in ends of rows, evenly sp 23 sc across, working in starting ch on opposite side of row 1, 3 sc in first ch, sc in each ch across with 3 sc in last ch, evenly sp 23 sc across ends of rows, join with sl st in first sc. Fasten off. *(104 sc)*

Sew Squares tog according to illustration A, making 2 strips of 2 by 3 Squares.

A

1	2
3	4
5	6

B

1	2
3	4
5	6

Sew "B" Squares 1 & 2 to "A" Squares 3 & 5 respectively *(see illustration B)*. Sew "B" Squares 3 & 5 to "A" Squares 1 & 2 respectively.

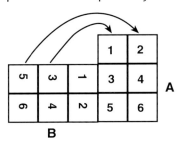

FINISHING
BOTTOM EDGE
Join with sc at bottom edge, sc evenly around in multiple of 4, working 3 sc in each corner, join with sl st in first sc. Fasten off.

FRINGE
Cut 1 strand of yarn 5 inches long. Fold strand in half, insert hook in st and pull fold through, pull ends through fold. Pull to tighten.

PEARL FRINGE
Cut 1 strand of yarn 5 inches long. Thread pearl on strand, fold strand in half with pearl at center of fold, insert hook in st and pull fold through, pull ends through fold. Pull to tighten.

Fringe in each st around bottom edge working pearl fringe on every fourth st.

NECK EDGE
Note: *Thread 27 pearls onto yarn before beg.*

Rnd 1: With RS facing, join at neck edge with sc, work 53 more sc around, join with sl st in first sc, turn. *(54 sc made)*

Rnd 2: Ch 1, sc in first st, pearl, [sc in next st, pearl] around, join. Fasten off.❏❏

Chenille Glamour

Design by Melissa Leapman

FINISHED SIZE
38 wide x 32 inches long

MATERIALS
- ❏ Lion Brand Chenille Thick and Quick bulky (chunky) weight yarn:
  32 oz/650 yds/960g #132 olive
- ❏ Size N/13/9mm crochet hook or size needed to obtain gauge
- ❏ Stitch markers

GAUGE
5-dc group = 2½ inches
Take time to check gauge.

INSTRUCTIONS
STRIP
Make 2.
BODY
Row 1 (RS): Ch 74, sc in 2nd ch from hook, *sk next 2 chs, 5 dc in next ch, sk next 2 chs, sc in next ch, rep from * across, turn.

Row 2: Ch 5 (*counts as a first dc and ch-2*), sk next 2 dc, *sc in next dc, ch 2, dc in next sc, ch 2, sk next 2 dc, rep from * 10 times, sc in next dc, ch 2, sk next 2 dc, dc in last sc, turn.

Row 3: Ch 1, sc in first dc, *5 dc in next sc, sc in next dc, rep from * 10 times, 5 dc in next sc, sc in last st, turn.

Next rows: Rep rows 2 and 3 alternately until strip measures about 21 inches from beg, ending with row 2. At end of last row, fasten off.

ASSEMBLY
Sew edges tog according to diagram. On lower edge, mark lp at front point and back point. On neck opening, mark each seam.

LOWER EDGING
Rnd 1: With RS facing and lower edge at top, join with sl st in 1 seam, ch 1, sc in same sp, *working along edge, evenly sp sc across to marked lp,

3 sc in marked lp (*corner made*), rep from * once, working along edge, evenly sp sc across to beg sc, join with sl st in beg sc.

Rnd 2: Ch 1, sc in first sc and in each sc across to 2nd sc of next corner, 3 sc in next sc (*corner made*), sc in each sc across to 2nd sc of next corner,

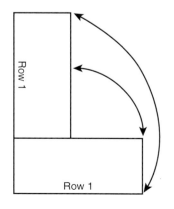

Row 1

Row 1

3 sc in next sc (*corner made*), sc in each sc across to first sc, join with sl st in beg sc. Fasten off.

NECK EDGING
Rnd 1: With RS facing and neck opening at top, join with sl st in ch-2 sp to left of 1 seam, ch 1, sc in same sp, working along edge in ch-2 sps, 2 sc in each ch-2 sp across to ch-2 sp before next seam, sc in next ch-2 sp (*mark this st*), sk seam, sc in next ch-2 sp, 2 sc in each ch-2 sp across to ch-2 sp before next seam, sc in next ch-2 sp (*mark this st*), join with sl st in beg sc.

Rnd 2: Ch 1, sc in first sc and in each sc across to next marked sc, **sc dec** (*see Stitch Guide*) in marked sc and next sc, sc in each sc across to next marked sc, sc dec in marked sc and in beg sc. Fasten off.❏❏

Montana Blue

Design by Mary Layfield

SKILL LEVEL
■■■□ INTERMEDIATE

FINISHED SIZE
One size fits most

MATERIALS
❑ Lion Brand Homespun bulky (chunky) weight yarn:
    30 oz/925 yds/850g #368 Montana sky
❑ Lion Brand Bouclé bulky (chunky) weight yarn:
    12½ oz/285 yds/350g #203 jelly bean
❑ Size K/10½/6.5mm crochet hook or size needed to obtain gauge
❑ Tapestry needle

GAUGE
3 dc = 1 inch, 3 dc rows = 2 inches
Take time to check gauge.

INSTRUCTIONS
FRONT SIDE
Make 2.
Row 1: With blue, ch 23, sc in 2nd ch from hook and in each ch across, turn. (22 sc made)

Row 2: Ch 3 (counts as first dc), dc in each of next 6 sts, hdc in next st, sc in each of next 13 sts, 2 sc in last st, turn. (23 sts)

Row 3: (Center front), ch 1, sc in each of first 8 sts, hdc in next st, [dc in each of next 3 sts, 2 dc in next st] 3 times, dc in each of last 2 sts, turn. (26 sts)

Row 4: Ch 3, dc in each of first 15 sts, hdc in next st, sc in each st across with 2 sc in last st, turn. (27 sts)

Row 5: (Ch 3, dc) in first st, 2 dc in next st, dc in each st across, turn. (29 dc)

Row 6: Ch 3, dc in each st across, turn.

Row 7: (Ch 3, dc) in first st, 2 dc in next st, dc in each st across, turn. Fasten off. (31 dc)

Row 8: Join jelly bean with sc in first st, sc in same st, sc in each of next 2 sts, * ch 1, sk next st, sc in each of next 2 sts, ch 1 sk next st**, sc in each of next 6 sts, rep from * across, ending last rep at **, sc in each of last 4 sts, turn. Fasten off. (26 sc, 6 ch sps)

Row 9: Join blue with sl st in first st, ch 3, 2 dc in next st, dc in each st and each ch across, for **first Side piece**, turn; for 2nd Side piece, do not turn. Fasten off for both pieces. (33 dc)

Row 10: Join jelly bean with sc in first st, sc in each of next 3 sts, * dtr in 2nd sk st 3 rows below, sk next st behind dtr, sc in each of next 2 sts, dtr in first sk st 3 rows below (cross st made), sk next st behind dtr**, sc in each of next 6 sts, rep from * across, ending last rep at **, sc in each st across, turn. (3 cross sts)

Row 11: (Center), join blue with sl st in first st, ch 3, dc in same st, dc in each st across with 2 dc in last st, turn. (35 dc)

Rows 12 & 13: Ch 3, dc in same st, dc in each st across with 2 dc in last st, turn. (37 dc, 39 dc)

Row 14: Ch 3, dc in each st across, turn.

Row 15: Rep row 12. (41 dc)

Row 16: Rep row 14.

Row 17: Rep row 12. (43 dc)

Row 18: Rep row 14.

Row 19: Rep row 12. Fasten off. (45 dc)

Row 20: Join jelly bean with sc in first st, sc in each of next 5 sts, ch 1, sk next st, sc in each of next 2 sts, ch 1, sk next st, [sc in each of next 6 sts, ch 1, sk next st, sc in each of next 2 sts, ch 1, sk next st] 3 times, sc in each of last 5 sts, turn. Fasten off.

Row 21: Join blue with sl st in first st, ch 3, dc in each st and ch across, turn. Fasten off.

Row 22: Join jelly bean with sc in first st, sc in each of next 5 sts, [*dtr in 2nd sk st on row 19, sk st behind dtr, sc in each of next 2 sts, dtr in first sk st on row 19, sk next st behind dtr*, sc in each of next 6 sts] 3 times, rep between * *, sc in each of last 5 sts, turn. Fasten off. (4 cross sts)

Row 23: Rep row 11. (47 dc)

Row 24: Rep row 12. (49 dc)

Row 25: Rep row 14.

Row 26: Rep row 12. (51 dc)

Row 27: Rep row 14.

Row 28: Rep row 12. (53 dc)

Row 29: Rep row 14.

Row 30: Rep row 12. (55 dc)

Row 31: Rep row 14. Fasten off.

Row 32: Join jelly bean with sc in first st, sc in each of next 5 sts, ch 1, sk next st, sc in each of next 2 sts, ch 1, sk next st, [sc in each of next 6 sts, ch 1, sk next st, sc in each of next 2 sts, ch 1, sk next st] 4 times, sc in each of last 5 sts, turn. Fasten off.

Row 33: Join blue with sl st in first st, ch 3, dc in each st and ch across, turn. Fasten off.

Row 34: Join jelly bean with sc in first st, sc in each of next 5 sts, [*dtr in 2nd sk st on row 31, sk st behind dtr, sc in each of next 2 sts, dtr in first sk st on row 31, sk next st behind dtr*, sc in each of next 6 sts] 4 times, rep between * *, sc in each of last 5 sts, turn. Fasten off. (5 cross sts)

Row 35: Rep row 12. (57 dc)

Row 36: Rep row 14.

Row 37: Rep row 12. (59 dc)

Row 38: Rep row 14.

Row 39: Rep row 12. (61 dc)

Row 40: Rep row 14.

Row 41: Rep row 12. (63 dc)

Row 42: Rep row 14.

Row 43: Rep row 12. Fasten off. (65 dc)

Sew center edges of Front Side pieces tog.

BACK SIDE
Make 2.
Row 1: With blue, ch 17, sc in 2nd ch from hook and in each ch across, turn. (16 sc made)

Row 2: (Center), ch 3, dc in same st, dc in each st across with 2 dc in last st, turn. (18 dc)

Row 3: Ch 3, dc in each of next 2 sts, 2 dc in next st, [dc in each of next

5 sts, 2 dc in next st] twice, dc in next st, 2 dc in last st, turn. *(22 dc)*

Row 4: Ch 3, dc in each of next 2 sts, 2 dc in next st, dc in each of next 5 sts, 2 dc in next st, dc in each st across, turn. *(24 dc)*

Row 5: Ch 3, dc in each of next 5 sts, 2 dc in next st, dc in each of next 8 sts, 2 dc in next st, dc in each st across, turn. *(26 dc)*

Row 6: Ch 3, dc in next st, 2 dc in next st, dc in each of next 6 sts, 2 dc in next st, dc in each of next 10 sts, 2 dc in next st, dc in each st across, turn. *(29 dc)*

Row 7: Ch 3, dc in each of next 20 sts, 2 dc in next st, dc in each of next 3 sts, 2 dc in next st, dc in each of last 3 sts, turn. Fasten off. *(31 dc)*

Rows 8–43: Rep rows 8–43 of Front Side.

Sew center edges of Back Side pieces tog.

Sew ends of rows 1–23 of Front to Back down each side edge.

FRINGE

Cut 2 strands jelly bean each 10 inches long. Hold both strands tog, fold in half, insert hook in st, pull fold through, pull ends through fold. Pull to tighten.

Fringe in each st around bottom edges. Trim ends.

NECK TRIM

Join jelly bean with sc at one shoulder seam, evenly sp sc around neck edge, join with sl st in beg sc. Fasten off.

TASSEL

Cut 13 strands of jelly bean each 10 inches long. Holding 12 strands tog, tie rem strand around center of strands. Fold strands in half, wrap rem strand from center several times around all strands 1 inch below fold. Tie and hide ends in tassel.

Sew Tassel to center Front as shown in photo.❏❏

Leaf Lace

Design by Melissa Leapman

SKILL LEVEL
■■■□ INTERMEDIATE

FINISHED SIZE
One size fits most

FINISHED MEASUREMENTS
Each panel measures approx 19 x 42 inches.

MATERIALS
- ❏ Cotton Classic 100 percent mercerized cotton medium (worsted) weight yarn from Tahki/Stacy Charles Inc. (108 yds/50g per ball): **4 MEDIUM**
    12 balls sunshine yellow #3534
- ❏ Size 6 (4mm) 29-inch circular needle or size needed to obtain gauge

GAUGE
21 sts and 28 rows = 4 inches/10cm in lace pat
To save time, take time to check gauge.

PATTERN NOTE
Circular needle is used to accommodate large number of sts. Do not join; work in rows.

PANEL
Make 2.
Cast on 186 sts.
Work even in garter st for 10 rows (5 ridges), ending with a WS row.
Referring to chart,

STITCH KEY
☐ K on RS, p on WS
⊟ P on RS, k on WS
○ Yo
⟍ Ssk
⟋ K2tog
⟑ Sl next 2 sts tog knitwise, k1, p2sso

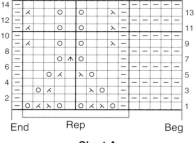

End   Rep   Beg

Chart A

work Rows 1–14 of lace pat until panel measures approx 17 inches from beg, ending with Row 14 of pat.
Work 10 rows of garter st.
Bind off.

ASSEMBLY
With RS facing, referring to Fig. 1, sew panels tog.❏❏

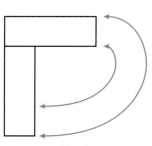

Fig. 1

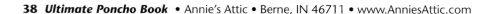

Pretty in Pink

Design by Eleanor Shnier

SKILL LEVEL
 EASY

FINISHED SIZE
Child 2–4 years old

MATERIALS
- ❑ Bernat Denim Style medium (worsted) weight yarn:
  - 7 oz/350 yds/198g #03426 weathered rose
  - 1 oz/50 yds/28g #03006 canvas
- ❑ Sizes J/10/6mm and P/15/10mm crochet hooks or size needed to obtain gauge
- ❑ Tapestry needle
- ❑ Ribbon rose with leaves

GAUGE
Size P hook: 5 hdc = 2 inches, 2 hdc rows = 1 inch
Take time to check gauge.

INSTRUCTIONS
Row 1 (RS): With size P hook and rose, ch 60 loosely, hdc in 3rd ch from hook *(first 2 chs count as hdc)* and in each ch across, turn. *(59 hdc made)*

Rows 2–11: Ch 2, hdc each st across, turn.

Row 12: Ch 2 *(counts as first st)*, hdc in each of next 15 sts, leaving rem sts unworked, turn. *(16 hdc)*

Rows 13–34: Ch 2, hdc in each st across, turn. At end of last row, fasten off.

Matching X's on illustration, sew row

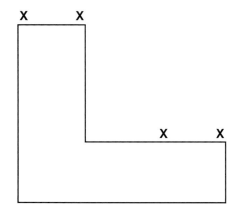

34 to sts on other end of row 11 *(see illustration)*.

NECK EDGING
Rnd 1: With RS facing and size J hook, join rose with sc in bottom of V at back, evenly sp sc around, join with sl st in first sc.

Rnds 2–3: Ch 1, sc in each st around, join. At end of last rnd, fasten off.

BORDER
Rnd 1: With RS facing and size J hook, join rose in point at back, evenly sp sc around in multiples of four, join with sl st in first sc.

Rnd 2: Ch 1, sc in each st around, join.

Rnd 3: Ch 1, sc in first st, sk next st, 5 dc in next st, sk next st, [sc in next st, sk next st, 5 dc in next st, sk next st] around, join. Fasten off.

FLOWER
With size J hook and canvas, ch 5, sl st in first ch to form ring, [ch 3, 3 tr, ch 3, sc] 6 times in ring, join with sl st in first ch of ch-3. Fasten off.

Sew Flower to V on Front as shown in photo. Tack ribbon rose in center of Flower. ❑❑

Purple Poetry

Design by Melissa Leapman

SKILL LEVEL

■■■□ INTERMEDIATE

FINISHED SIZE

42 x 26 inches long

MATERIALS

❏ Lion Brand Chenille Sensations medium (worsted) weight yarn: 19 oz/1150 yds/ 540g #145 violet

❏ Size H/8/5mm crochet hook or size needed to obtain gauge

❏ Tapestry needle

[4 MEDIUM]

GAUGE

6 shells = 4 inches, 9 rows = 4 inches
Take time to check gauge.

INSTRUCTIONS

PONCHO

BACK

Row 1 (WS): Ch 5, dc in 5th ch from hook *(first 4 chs count as first dc and ch-1)*, turn.

Row 2 (RS): Ch 3 *(counts as first dc throughout)*, dc in same dc, 3 dc in ch sp, 2 dc in last st, turn.

Row 3: Ch 4 *(counts as first dc and ch sp)*, dc in same st, sk next 2 dc, (dc, ch 1, dc) in next st, sk next 2 dc, (dc, ch 1, dc) in last st, turn.

Row 4: Ch 3, dc in same dc, *3 dc in each ch-1 sp across with 2 dc in last st, turn.

Row 5: Ch 4, dc in first dc, *sk next 2 dc, (dc, ch 1, dc) in next dc, rep from * across turn.

Rows 6–47: Rep rows 4 and 5 alternately 19 times.

Row 48: Rep row 4.

NECK SHAPING

LEFT SIDE

Row 1 (WS): Ch 4, dc in same dc, *sk next 2 dc, (dc, ch 1, dc) in next dc, rep from * 17 times, sk next 2 dc, dc in next dc leaving rem sts unworked, turn.

Row 2 (RS): Ch 3, 3 dc in each of next 18 ch-1 sps, 2 dc in last st. Fasten off.

RIGHT SIDE

Row 1 (WS): With WS facing, sk next 29 unworked dc on row 48, join with sl st in next dc, ch 3 *(counts as first dc)*, *sk next 2 dc, (dc, ch 1, dc) in next dc, rep from * across, turn.

Row 2 (RS): Ch 3, dc in first dc, 3 dc in each of next 19 ch-1 sps, sk next dc, dc in last st. Fasten off.

EDGING

Row 1 (RS): With RS facing, join with sl st in end of last row on left side, ch 1, sc in same sp, working along side in ends of rows, 2 sc in each row across, 5 sc in unworked lp of beg ch-5 of piece, working along next side in ends of rows, 2 sc in each row across to last row of right side, sc in end of last row, turn. *(203 sc)*

Row 2: Ch 4, sk first 2 sc, *dc in next sc, ch 1, sk next sc*, rep between * 48 times, [dc in next sc, ch 1] 3 times, sk next sc, rep between * 49 times, dc in last sc, turn.

Row 3: Ch 1, (sc, ch 2, sc) in each ch-1 sp across. Fasten off.

FRONT

Work same as Back through row 44.

NECK SHAPING

RIGHT SIDE

Row 1 (WS): Ch 4, dc in same dc, [sk next 2 dc, (dc, ch 1, dc) in next dc] 16 times, sk next dc, dc in next dc leaving rem sts unworked, turn.

Row 2 (RS): Ch 3, 3 dc in each of ch-1 sp across with 2 dc in last st, turn.

Row 3: Ch 4, dc in same dc, [sk next 2 dc, (dc, ch 1, dc) in next dc] 17 times, sk next dc, dc in last dc, turn.

Row 4: Ch 3, 3 dc in each ch-1 sp across, 2 dc in last st, turn.

Row 5: Ch 4, dc in same dc, [sk next 2 dc, (dc, ch 1, dc) in next dc] 18 times, sk next dc, dc in last dc, turn.

Row 6: Ch 3, 3 dc in each ch-1 sp across, 2 dc in last st. Fasten off.

LEFT SIDE

Row 1 (WS): With WS facing, sk next 28 unworked dc on row 44 from Right Side, join with sl st in next dc, ch 3, sk next dc, (dc, ch 1, dc) in next dc, *sk next 2 dc, (dc, ch 1, dc) in next dc, rep from * 14 times, sk next 2 dc, (dc, ch 1, dc) in last st, turn.

Row 2 (RS): Ch 3, dc in same dc, 3 dc in each of next 17 ch-1 sps, sk next dc, dc in last st, turn.

Row 3: Ch 3, sk next dc, (dc, ch 1, dc) in next dc, *sk next 2 dc, (dc, ch 1, dc) in next dc, rep from * 15 times, sk next 2 dc, (dc, ch 1, dc) in last st, turn.

Row 4: Ch 3, dc in same dc, 3 dc in each of next 18 ch-1 sps, sk next dc, dc last st, turn.

Row 5: Ch 3, sk next dc, (dc, ch 1, dc) in next dc, *sk next 2 dc, (dc, ch 1, dc) in next dc, rep from * 16 times, sk next 2 dc, (dc, ch 1, dc) in last st, turn.

Row 6: Ch 3, dc in same dc, 3 dc in each of next 19 ch-1 sps, sk next dc, dc in last st. Fasten off.

EDGING

Work same as Edging for Back.

ASSEMBLY

Sew shoulder seams.

NECKBAND

Rnd 1 (RS): Hold Poncho with RS facing, join with sl st in left shoulder seam, ch 1, sc in same sp, working along front neck edge in ends of rows, evenly sp sc across to row 1 of left side, **sc dec** *(see Stitch Guide)* in row 1 and next unworked dc of row 44 of front, evenly sp sc across front to last unworked dc, sc dec in last unworked dc and row 1 of right side, working along right side and back, evenly sp sc around to first sc, join with sl st in beg sc.

Rnd 2: Ch 1, sc in first sc and in each sc around, join with sl st in beg sc. Fasten off.❏❏

Embossed Fans

Design by Paula Clark

FINISHED SIZE
One size fits most

MATERIALS
- ❏ J. & P. Coats Knit-Cro-Sheen size 10 crochet cotton (150 yds per ball):
    - 10 balls #25 crystal blue
- ❏ YLI Candlelight Metallic yarn (125 yds per cone):
    - 450 yds #040 royal blue
- ❏ Size 6/1.80mm steel crochet hook or size needed to obtain gauge
- ❏ Pearl beads: 156 white 5mm
- ❏ White sewing thread
- ❏ Sewing needle

GAUGE
Motif is 2½ inches across.
Take time to check gauge.

SPECIAL STITCH
Roll stitch (roll st): Yo 12 times, insert hook as indicated, yo and pull lp through, yo, pull through all lps on hook, ch 1 to secure.

INSTRUCTIONS

FIRST MOTIF
Rnd 1: With crystal blue, [ch 4, dc in 4th ch from hook] 4 times, join with sl st in first ch of first ch-4. *(4 dc, 4 ch sps made)*

Rnd 2: Ch 1, sc in same ch, [ch 1, 5 **roll sts** *(see Special Stitch)* in next ch sp, sc in base of next dc] 3 times, ch 1, 5 roll sts in next ch sp, join with sl st in first sc. *(20 rolls sts)*

Rnd 3: Sl st in next roll st, ch 1, (sc, ch 1, sc) in same st, (sc, ch 1, sc) in each of next 4 roll sts, ch 7, *(sc, ch 1, sc) in each of next 5 roll sts, ch 7, rep from * around, join with sl st in first sc.

Rnd 4: Ch 1, *(sc, ch 2) in each of next 2 ch-1 sps, (sc, ch 3, sc) in next ch-1 sp, (ch 2, sc) in each of next 2 ch-1 sps, (sc, ch 2, sc, ch 3, sc, ch 5, sc, ch 3, sc, ch 2, sc) in next ch-7 sp, rep from * around, join. Fasten off.

NEXT MOTIF
Rnd 1: With crystal blue, [ch 4, dc in 4th ch from hook] 4 times, join with sl st in first ch of first ch-4. *(4 dc, 4 ch sps made)*

Rnd 2: Ch 1, sc in same ch, [ch 1, 5 roll sts in next ch sp, sc in base of next dc] 3 times, ch 1, 5 roll sts in next ch sp, join with sl st in first sc.

Rnd 3: Sl st in next roll st, ch 1, (sc, ch 1, sc) in same st, (sc, ch 1, sc) in each of next 4 roll sts, ch 7, *(sc, ch 1, sc) in each of next 5 roll sts, ch 7, rep from * around, join with sl st in first sc.

Rnd 4: Joining rnd, ch 1, (sc, ch 2) in each of next 2 ch-1 sps, (sc, ch 3, sc) in next ch-1 sp, (ch 2, sc) in each of next 2 ch-1 sps, *(sc, ch 2, sc, ch 3, sc, ch 2, sl st) in ch-5 sp on previous Motif, ch 2, (sc, ch 3, sc, ch 2, sc) in next ch-7 sp**, (sc, ch 2) in each of next 2 ch-1 sps, (sc, ch 1, sl st in ch-3 sp of previous Motif, ch 1, sc) in next ch-1 sp, (ch 2, sc) in each of next 2 ch-1 sps*, rep from * to **, rep between * * across sides as many times needed to join Motifs tog ending last rep at **, [(sc, ch 2) in each of next 2 ch-1 sps, (sc, ch 1, sc) in next ch-1 sp, (ch 2, sc) in each of next 2 ch-1 sps, (sc, ch 2, sc, ch 3, sc, ch 5, sc, ch 3, sc, ch 2, sc) in next ch-7 sp] around, join. Fasten off.

Make a total of 130 Motifs, joining according to illustration, joining last Motifs not only to last row, but to side of first rows between X's as indicated on illustration.

NECK EDGING
Rnd 1: Join crystal blue with sl st in joining at V in back, ch 4 *(counts as first tr)*, tr in same joining, *[ch 5, sk next 4 ch sps, (sc, ch 3, sc) in next ch-3 sp, ch 5, (2 tr, ch 3, 2 tr) in next joining] 7 times, ch 5, sk next 4 ch sps, (sc, ch 3, sc) in next ch-3 sp, ch 5*, 2 tr in next joining *(front V)*, rep

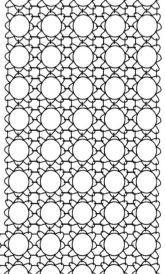

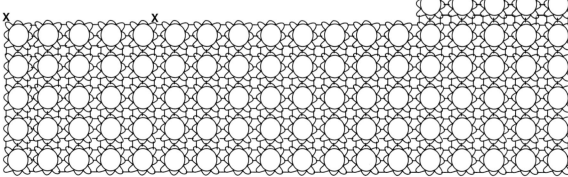

between * *, join with sl st in 4th ch of beg ch-4.

Rnd 2: Sl st between tr, ch 1, sc in same sp, *[ch 1, 5 dc in 3rd ch of ch-5 sp, ch 1, sc in next ch-3 sp] 15 times, 5 dc in 3rd ch of ch-5 sp, ch 1*, sc between next 2 tr, rep between * *, join with sl st in first sc.

Rnd 3: Ch 1, (sc, ch 2, sc) in first st, [sk next st, (sc, ch 2, sc) in next st] around, join. Fasten off.

FLOWER
Make 156.
Rnd 1: With royal blue, ch 5, sl st in first ch to form ring, ch 1, 12 sc in ring, join with sl st in first sc. *(12 sc made)*

Rnd 2: Ch 1, sc in first st, ch 3, sk next st, [sc in next st, ch 3, sk next st] around, join.

Rnd 3: Ch 1, (sc, hdc, 3 dc, hdc, sc) in each ch sp around, join. Fasten off.

Sew one bead to center of each Flower and sew Flower over each corner joining and point of Poncho as shown in photo.

FRINGE
Cut 144 royal blue 10-inch strands. Holding 4 strands tog, fold in half, insert hook in joining or point pull fold through, pull ends through fold. Tighten.

Fringe over joinings and at points around bottom edge.

TIE
With crystal blue, make a ch 45 inches long, sl st in each ch across. Fasten off.

Starting in the ch-1 sp to the left of front V, weave tie behind 5-dc groups and over sc around neck edge. Tie ends in bow at Front.❏❏

Southwest Serape

Design by Melissa Leapman

SKILL LEVEL
■■■□ INTERMEDIATE

FINISHED SIZE
42 inches wide x 25 inches long

MATERIALS
- Medium (worsted) weight yarn:
  - 27 oz/1773 yds/810g coral
  - 3 oz/197 yds/90g green
- Sizes H/8/5mm and I/9/5.5mm crochet hooks or size needed to obtain gauge
- Tapestry needle
- 15½ x 6 inch piece of cardboard *(for tassels)*

GAUGE
Size H hook: 12 sts in pattern = 4 inches, 16 rows = 4 inches
Take time to check gauge.

PATTERN NOTE
Each chain-1 space counts as stitch.

INSTRUCTIONS
SERAPE
BACK
Row 1 (WS): With size I hook and green, ch 128, sc in 2nd ch from hook and in next ch, [ch 1, sk next ch, sc in next ch] across with sc in last ch, turn.

Row 2 (RS): Ch 1, sc in first sc, *ch 1, sk next sc, sc in next ch-1 sp, rep from * across to last 2 sc, ch 1, sk next sc, sc in last sc, turn.

Row 3: Ch 1, sc in first sc, *sc in next ch-1 sp, ch 1, sk next sc, rep from * across to last ch-1 sp, sc in last ch-1 sp and in last sc, turn.

Rows 4 & 5: Rep rows 2 and 3. At end of last row, **change color** *(see Stitch Guide)* to coral in last st. Fasten off green.

Row 6: Rep row 2 changing to green in last st. Fasten off coral.

Row 7: Rep row 3.

Rows 8–11: Rep rows 2 and 3 alternately twice. At end of last row, change to coral in last st. Fasten off green.

Rows 12–83: Rep rows 6–11 consecutively 12 times.

Rows 84–87: Rep rows 6–9.

SHOULDER SHAPING
FIRST SHOULDER
Row 1 (RS): Ch 1, sc in first sc, *ch 1, sk next sc, sc in next ch-1 sp, rep from * 27 times leaving rem sts unworked, turn.

Row 2: Ch 1, **sc dec** *(see Stitch Guide)* in first sc and next ch-1 sp, *ch 1, sk next sc, sc in next ch-1 sp, rep from * 26 times, sc in last sc, turn.

Row 3: Ch 1, sc in first sc, *ch 1, sk next sc, sc in next ch-1 sp, rep from * 25 times, ch 1, sk next sc, sc dec in next ch-1 sp and last st. changing to green, turn. Fasten off coral.

Row 4: Ch 1, sc dec in first st and next ch-1 sp, *ch 1, sk next sc, sc in next ch-1 sp, rep from * 25 times, sc in last sc, turn.

Row 5: Ch 1, sc in first sc, *ch 1, sk next sc, sc in next ch-1 sp, rep from * 24 times, ch 1, sk next sc, sc dec in next ch-1 sp and next st, turn.

Row 6: Ch 1, sc in first sc and in next ch-1 sp, *ch 1, sk next sc, sc in next ch-1 sp, rep from * 24 times, sc in last sc, turn.

Row 7: Ch 1, sc in first sc, *ch 1, sk next sc, sc in next ch-1 sp, rep from * 24 times, ch 1, sk next sc, sc in last sc. Fasten off.

SECOND SHOULDER
Row 1 (RS): Hold piece with RS facing, sk next 13 unworked sts on row 87 from First Shoulder Shaping, join green with sl st in next ch-1 sp, ch 1, sc in same sp, *ch 1, sk next sc, sc in next ch-1 sp, rep from * 27 times, ch 1, sk next sc, sc in next sc, turn.

Row 2: Ch 1, sc in first sc and in next ch-1 sp, *ch 1, sk next sc, sc in next ch-1 sp, rep from * 25 times, sc dec in next ch-1 sp and last sc, changing to coral, turn. Fasten off green.

Row 3: Ch 1, sc dec in first st and next ch-1 sp, *ch 1, sk next sc, sc in next ch-1 sp, rep from * 25 times, ch 1,

sk next sc, sc in last sc changing to green, turn. Fasten off coral.

Row 4: Ch 1, sc in first sc and in next ch-1 sp, *ch 1, sk next sc, sc in next ch-1 sp, rep from * 24 times, ch 1, sk next sc, sc dec in next ch-1 sp and last st, turn.

Row 5: Ch 1, sc dec in first st and next ch-1 sp, *ch 1, sk next sc, sc in next ch-1 sp, rep from * 24 times, ch 1, sk next sc, sc in last sc, turn.

Row 6: Ch 1, sc in first sc and in next ch-1 sp, *ch 1, sk next sc, sc in next ch-1 sp, rep from * 24 times, sc in last sc, turn.

Row 7: Ch 1, sc in first sc, *ch 1, sk next sc, sc in next ch-1 sp, rep from * 24 times, ch 1, sk next sc, sc in last sc. Fasten off.

FRONT
Rows 1–83: Work rows 1–83 of Back.

Rows 84–89: Rep rows 6–11 of Back.

Rows 90 & 91: Rep rows 6 and 7 of Back.

SHOULDER SHAPING
FIRST SHOULDER
Row 1 (RS): Ch 1, sc in first sc, *ch 1, sk next sc, sc in next ch-1 sp, rep from * 25 times leaving rem sts unworked, turn,

Row 2: Ch 1, sc in first sc and in next ch-1 sp, *ch 1, sk next sc, sc in next ch-1 sp, rep from * 24 times, sc in last sc, turn.

Row 3: Ch 1, sc in first sc, *ch 1, sk next sc, sc in next ch-1 sp, rep from * 25 times. Fasten off.

SECOND SHOULDER
Row 1 (RS): Hold Serape with RS facing, sk next 21 unworked sts on row 91 from First Shoulder Shaping, join green with sl st in next ch-1 sp, ch 1, sc in same sp, *ch 1, sk next sc, sc in next ch-1 sp, rep from * 24 times, ch 1, sk next sc, sc in next sc, turn.

Row 2: Ch 1, sc in first sc and in next ch-1 sp, *ch 1, sk next sc, sc in next ch-1 sp, rep from * 24 times, sc in last sc, turn.

Row 3: Ch 1, sc in first sc, *ch 1, sk next sc, sc in next ch-1 sp, rep from * 24 times, ch 1, sk next sc, sc in last sc. Fasten off.

ASSEMBLY
Sew shoulder seams.

NECK EDGING
Hold Serape with RS facing and neck opening at top, with green and size H hook, join with sc in left shoulder seam, working in ends of rows, sc in each of next 7 rows, working across Front, sc in each ch-1 sp and in each sc, working along next side in ends of rows, sc in each of next 7 rows, in seam, and in each of next 3 rows, working across Back, sc in each ch-1 sp and in each sc, working across next side, sc in each of next 3 rows, join with sl st in beg sc. Fasten off.

NECKBAND
Row 1: With size H hook and green, ch 17, sc in 2nd ch from hook and in each ch across, turn.
Row 2: Working in **back lps** (see Stitch Guide) only, ch 1, sc in each sc across, turn.
Next rows: Rep row 2 until piece measures 14 inches (when slightly stretched piece fits around neckline). At end of last row, fasten off.

TASSEL
Make 4.
Wind green loosely and evenly lengthwise around cardboard. Cut yarn across 1 end. Fold 21 strands in half over additional strand (used to attach tassel), wrap another strand loosely around all doubled strands, about 2½ inches from fold, wrapping 9 times and knotting at back of tassel. Trim ends evenly. Rep for rem tassels.

FINISHING
Step 1: With tapestry needle and green, sew first and last rows of Neckband tog through back lps only. Sew Neckband to neckline, placing seam at center back.
Step 2: Sew tassels to 4 lower corners of Serape.❏❏

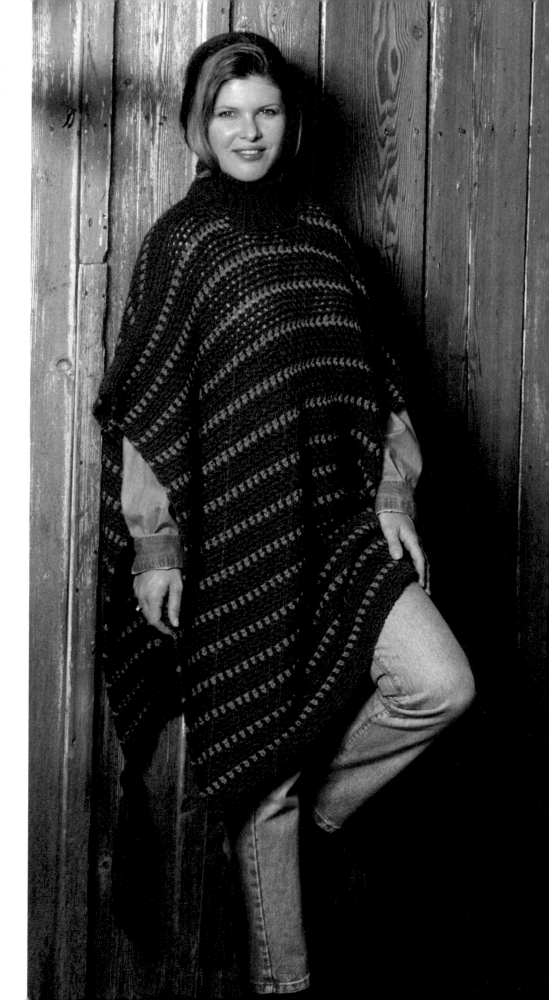

Yin & Yang

Design by George Shaheen

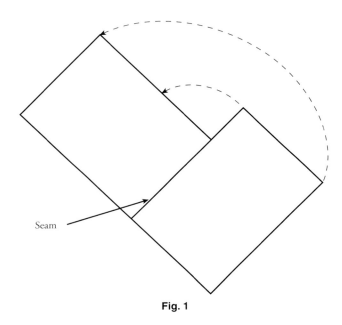

SKILL LEVEL
■■□□ EASY

FINISHED SIZES
Small/medium (large/extra-large) Instructions are given for smallest size, with larger sizes in parentheses. When only 1 number is given, it applies to all sizes.

MATERIALS
❑ Cotton-Ease 50 percent cotton/50 percent acrylic medium (worsted) weight yarn from Lion Brand (207 yds/100g per skein):
   1 skein each orangeade #133 (A), and candy blue #107 (B)
❑ Size 10½ (6.5mm) straight needles or size needed to obtain gauge

GAUGE
12 sts = 4 inches/10cm in openwork pat
To save time, take time to check gauge.

PATTERN STITCH
OPENWORK
Rows 1 and 3 (WS): K1, purl to last st, k1.
Row 2 (RS): K1, *k2tog, yo; rep from * to last 2 sts, k2.
Row 4: K2, *yo, ssk; rep from * to last st, k1.
Rep Rows 1 – 4 for pat.

PANEL NO. 1
With A, cast on 71 (79) sts.
Rep Rows 1–4 of Openwork pat in following color sequence: 3 rows A, 2 rows B, 6 rows A, 2 rows B, 6 rows A, 2 rows B, 3 rows A.
Work even in established pat until panel measures approx 8 ½ (9) inches, ending with Row 1 or 3 of pat.
Knit 2 rows.
Bind off.

PANEL NO. 2
With B, cast on 71 (79) sts.
Rep Rows 1–4 of Openwork pat in following color sequence: 3 rows B, 2 rows A, 6 rows B, 2 rows A, 6 rows B, 2 rows A, 3 rows B.
Work even in established pat until panel measures approx 8½ (9) inches, ending with Row 1 or 3 of pat.
Knit 2 rows.
Bind off.

ASSEMBLY
Block pieces to measure 24 x 9 (26 x 9½) inches.
Referring to Fig. 1, sew pieces tog.❑❑

Seam

Fig. 1

Retro-spect Granny

Design by Zena Low for Lily

SKILL LEVEL
■■□□ EASY

FINISHED SIZE
One size fits most

MATERIALS
❑ Lily Sugar 'n Cream medium (worsted) weight cotton yarn: (2½ oz/120 yds/70g per ball):
  4 balls #82 jute
  4 balls #09 bright navy
  3 balls #1130 warm brown
  1 ball #04 ecru
  1 ball #26 light blue
❑ Size G/6/4mm crochet hook or size needed to obtain gauge
❑ Tapestry needle

GAUGE
Each Motif is 4 inches square.
Take time to check gauge.

COLOR SEQUENCE
Motif No. 1
Make 12.
Use ecru for first color, brown as 2nd color, navy as 3rd color and jute as 4th color.

Motif No. 2
Make 8.
Use blue as first color, navy as 2nd color, brown as 3rd color and jute as 4th color.

Motif No. 3
Make 10.
Use ecru as first color, navy as 2nd color, brown as 3rd color and jute as 4th color.

Motif No. 4
Make 12.
Use blue as first color, brown as 2nd color, navy as 3rd color and jute as 4th color.

INSTRUCTIONS
MOTIF
Rnd 1: With first color, ch 4, sl st in first ch to form ring, ch 3 (counts as first dc), 2 dc in ring, [ch 1, 3 dc in ring] 3 times, ch 1, join with sl st in 3rd ch of beg ch-3. Fasten off. (12 dc, 4 ch sps made)

Rnd 2: Join 2nd color with sl st in any ch sp, ch 3, (2 dc, ch 1, 3 dc) in same ch sp, (3 dc, ch 1, 3 dc) in each ch sp (corner made) around, join. Fasten off. (24 dc, 4 ch sps)

Rnd 3: Join 3rd color with sl st in any corner ch sp, ch 3, (2 dc, ch 1, 3 dc) in same sp, 3 dc in next sp between dc group, [(3 dc, ch 1, 3 dc) in next corner ch sp, 3 dc in next sp between dc-groups] around, join. Fasten off. (36 dc, 4 ch sps)

Rnd 4: Join 4th color with sl st in any corner ch sp, (ch 3, 2 dc, ch 1, 3 dc) in same sp, 3 dc in each sp between dc-groups, [(3 dc, ch 1, 3 dc) in next corner ch sp, 3 dc in each sp between dc-groups] around, join. Fasten off. (48 dc, 4 ch sps)

Sew Motifs tog according to illustration, making front and back the same.

Sew front and back tog at shoulder seams.

NECK EDGING
Rnd 1: Join jute with sl st at shoulder seam, ch 1, sc in each dc around and **sc dec** (see Stitch Guide) in next 2 sts at V in front and back, join with sl st in first sc. Fasten off.

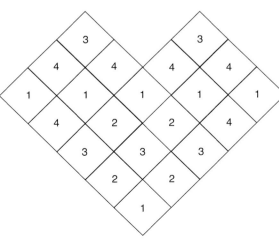

Poncho Diagram

Rnd 2: Join ecru with sc in first st, [sk next st, ch 1, sc in next st] around with sc dec in next 2 sts at V in front and back, join with sl st in first st. Fasten off.

Rnd 3: Join navy with sc in first st, [sc in sk st on rnd 1, ch 1, sk next st] around with sc dec in next 2 sts at V in front and back, join. Fasten off.

TIE
With jute, make chain 60 inches long, working in **back bar of chs** (see illustration), sl st in 2nd ch from hook and in each ch across. Fasten off.

Back Bar of Ch

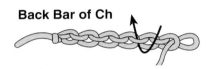

Beg at center front, weave tie through last rnd of Neck Edging. Tie ends in bow.

BOTTOM EDGING
Rnd 1: Join jute with sl st at bottom of shoulder seam, sc in each dc around with 3 sc in each point, join with sl st in first sc.

Rnd 2: Ch 1, sc in each st around with 3 sc in each point, join. Fasten off.

Rnd 3: Join ecru with sc in first st, sk next st, ch 2, [sc in next st, ch 2, sk next st] around with 3 sc in each point, join. Fasten off.

Rnd 4: Join navy with sc in first sk st of rnd 2, ch 1, sk next st on last row, [sc in next sk st on rnd 2, ch 1, sk next st on last rnd] around with 3 sc in each point, join. Fasten off.

FRINGE
Cut 3 strands of yarn each 14 inches long. Holding 3 strands tog, fold in half, insert hook in st, pull fold through, pull ends through fold. Pull to tighten.

Beg at point, work [3 navy fringes and 1 brown fringe] around. Trim ends.❑❑

Colorful Stripes

Design by Tammy Hildebrand

SKILL LEVEL
■■■◻ INTERMEDIATE

FINISHED SIZES
Instructions are given for 7–8 (small), changes for 10–12 (medium) and 14–16 (large)are in [ ]

MATERIALS
❑ Medium (worsted) weight yarn (3.5 oz/175 yds/99g per skein):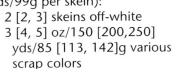
    2 [2, 3] skeins off-white
    3 [4, 5] oz/150 [200,250] yds/85 [113, 142]g various scrap colors
❑ Size J/10/6mm crochet hook or size needed to obtain gauge
❑ Tapestry needle

GAUGE
3 dc = 1 inch, 3 rows = 2 inches
Take time to check gauge.

SPECIAL STITCHES
Cross-stitch (cross st): Sk next st, dc in next st, dc in sk st.

Beginning cross-stitch (beg cross-st): Ch 3 (counts as first dc), dc in previous st.

INSTRUCTIONS
PONCHO
Rnd 1 (RS): Starting at neckline, with off-white, ch 56 [68, 80] dc in 4th ch from hook (first 3 chs count as first dc), dc in each of next 6 [8, 10] chs, (dc, ch 2, dc) in next ch, [dc in each of next 8 [10, 12] chs, (dc, ch 2, dc) in next ch] 5 times, join with sl st in 3rd ch of beg ch-3. (6 ch-2 points)

Rnd 2: Beg cross-st (see Special Stitches), [**cross-st** (see Special Stitches) in each of next 2 sts across to next ch-2 sp, (2 dc, ch 2, 2 dc) in next ch-2 sp] 6 times, join with sl st in 3rd ch of beg ch-3. Fasten off.

Rnd 3: Join color with sl st in any ch-2 sp, ch 1, (sc, ch 2, sc) in same ch-2 sp, working in sps before each cross-st, (sc, ch 3) in each sp, sc in sp before next 2 sts, [(sc, ch 2, sc) in next ch-2 sp, (sc, ch 3) in sp before each cross-st across, sc in sp before next 2 sts] around, join with sl st in beg sc. Fasten off.

Rnd 4: Join off-white with sl st in any ch-2 sp, ch 3 (counts as first dc), (dc, ch 2, 2 dc) in same ch-2 sp, 2 dc in each ch-3 sp across edge, [(2 dc, ch 2, 2 dc) in next ch-2 sp, 2 dc in each ch-3 sp across] around, join with sl st in 3rd ch of beg ch-3.

Next rnds: Rep rnds 2–4 8 [10, 12] times.

Next rnds: Rep rnds 2 and 3.

BOTTOM TRIM
Join off-white with sl st in any ch-2 sp, ch 3, 6 dc in same ch-2 sp, [sc in next ch-3 sp, {5 dc in next ch-3 sp, sc in next ch-3 sp} across to next ch-2 sp, 7 dc in next ch-2 sp] 5 times, sc in next ch-3 sp, [5 dc in next ch-3 sp, sc in next ch-3 sp] around, join with sl st in 3rd ch of beg ch-3. Fasten off.

NECKLINE TRIM
Join off-white with sl st in starting ch on opposite side of rnd 1, ch 1, sc in same ch, ch 1, [sc in next ch, ch 1] around, join with sl st in beg sc. Fasten off.❑❑

Lavender Dreams

Design by Margaret Hubert

SKILL LEVEL
■■■□ INTERMEDIATE

FINISHED SIZE
Girls size 6–8 (small)
Neckline to bottom edge measures
18 inches

MATERIALS
❏ Patons Grace cotton
light (sport) weight
yarn (1¾ oz/
136 yds/50g per skein):
  7 skeins #60321 lilac
  3 skeins #60903 lavender
  2 skeins #60005 snow
❏ Size E/4/305mm crochet hook
or size needed to obtain gauge
❏ Size D/3/3.25mm crochet hook
for border only

GAUGE
Size E hook: Square = 3¾ inches; 7 dc =
1½ inches
Take time to check gauge.

PATTERN NOTES
Make 60 Squares as indicated.
Size E hook is used throughout unless
otherwise specified.

SPECIAL STITCHES
Cluster (cl): [Yo, insert hook in ch sp,
yo, pull up lp, yo, pull through 2 lps
on hook] 3 times in same ch sp, yo,
pull through all lps on hook.
Popcorn (pc): 5 dc in indicated st,
drop lp from hook, insert hook in
first dc of 5-dc group, pull dropped
lp through st.

INSTRUCTIONS
SQUARE 1
**Make 8 with rnds 1–3 lilac, rnds
4–6 are indicated in pattern.**
**Make 4 with rnds 1–3 snow, rnds
4–6 are indicated in pattern.**
Rnd 1: Ch 8, sl st in first ch to form
ring, ch 1, 16 sc in ring, join with sl
st in beg sc. (16 sc made)
Rnd 2: Ch 6 (counts as first dc and
ch-3), sk next sc, [dc in next sc, ch

3, sk next sc] around, join with sl st
in 3rd ch of beg ch-6. (8 ch-3 sps)
Rnd 3: Ch 1, (sc, hdc, 2 dc, hdc, sc)
in each ch-3 sp around, join with sl
st in beg sc. Fasten off.
Rnd 4: Pull up lp of lavender in last st
of previous rnd, ch 3 (counts as first
dc), [ch 5, sc between next 2 dc]
twice, ch 5, *dc between next 2 sc,
[ch 5, sc between next 2 dc] twice,
ch 5, rep from * around, join with
sl st in 3rd ch of beg ch-3.
Rnd 5: Ch 3, dc in same st, ch 1, (3 dc,
ch 1) in each of next 3 ch-5 sps, *(2 dc,
ch 2, 2 dc) in next dc, ch 1, (3 dc, ch
1) in each of next 3 ch-5 sps, rep from
* around, ending with 2 dc in same
sp as beg ch-3, ch 2, join with sl st in
3rd ch of beg ch-3. Fasten off.
Rnd 6: Join lilac with sl st in top of beg
ch-3 of previous rnd, ch 1, sc in each
dc and in each ch-1 sp around, with
3 sc in each corner ch-2 sp, join with
sl st in beg sc. Fasten off.

Square 1

SQUARE 2
Make 3 with rnds 1–6 lilac.
**Make 4 with rnd 1 lilac, rnds 2–5
lavender and rnd 6 lilac.**
**Make 5 with rnd 1 lilac, rnds 2–5
snow and rnd 6 lilac.**
Rnd 1: Ch 4, sl st in first ch to form
ring, ch 1, 8 sc in ring, join with sl
st in beg sc. (8 sc made)
Rnd 2: Pull up a long lp, [yo, insert hook
in same st, yo, pull up another long
lp] 4 times, yo, pull through all lps on

hook, ch 3, *yo, insert hook in next sc,
yo, pull up a long lp, [yo, insert hook in
same st, yo, pull up a long lp] 3 times,
yo, pull through all lps on hook, ch
3, rep from * 6 times, join with sl st in
3rd ch of beg st. Fasten off.
Rnd 3: Join next color with sl st in any
ch-3 sp, ch 3, (dc, ch 2, 2 dc) in same
sp, 4 dc in next ch-3 sp, *(2 dc, ch
2, 2 dc) in next ch-3 sp, 4 dc in next
ch-3 sp, rep from * around, join with
sl st in 3rd ch of beg ch-3.
Rnd 4: Ch 3, dc in next dc, (dc, ch
2, dc) in next ch-2 sp, *dc in each
of next 8 dc, (dc, ch 2, dc) in next
ch-2 sp, rep from * around, ending
with dc in each of last 6 dc, join with
sl st in 3rd ch of beg ch-3.
Rnd 5: Ch 3, dc in each of next 2 dc,
*(dc, ch 2, dc) in corner ch-2 sp,
dc in each of next 10 dc, rep from
* around, ending with dc in each of
last 7 dc, join with sl st in 3rd ch of
beg ch-3. Fasten off.
Rnd 6: Join lilac with sl st in last st of
previous rnd, ch 1, sc in each st around,
working 5 sc in each corner ch-2 sp,
join with sl st in beg sc. Fasten off.

Square 2

SQUARE 3
Make 5 with rnds 1–6 lilac.
**Make 5 with rnds 1–3 lilac, rnds
4 & 5 snow and rnd 6 lilac.**
Rnd 1: Ch 3, sl st in first ch to form
ring, ch 3, 15 dc in ring, join with
sl st in 3rd ch of beg ch-3.
Rnd 2: Ch 5 (counts as first dc and ch 2),

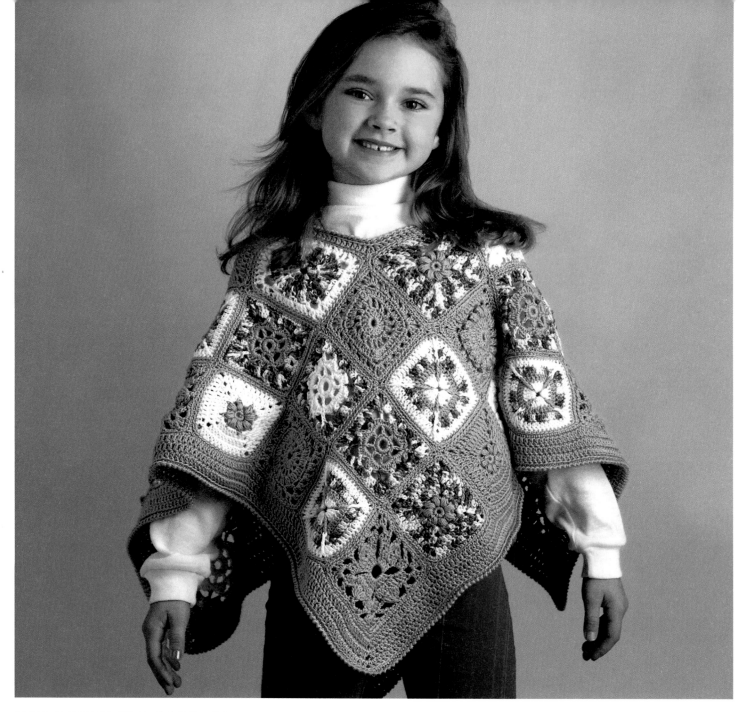

Square 3

*(dc, ch 2) in next dc, rep from * around, join with sl st in 3rd ch of beg ch-5.

Rnd 3: Sl st into ch-2 sp, ch 3, 2 dc in same ch-2 sp, ch 1, (3 dc, ch 1) in each ch-2 sp around, join with sl st in 3rd ch of beg ch-3.

Rnd 4: Sl st into ch-1 sp, ch 1, sc in same ch-1 sp, *[ch 3, sc in next ch-1 sp] 3 times, ch 6, sc in next ch-1 sp, rep from * around, join with sl st in beg sc.

Rnd 5: Sl st into ch-3 sp, ch 3, 2 dc in same ch-3 sp, 3 dc in each of next 2 ch-3 sps, *(2 dc, ch 2, 2 dc) in next ch-6 sp, 3 dc in each of next 3 ch-3 sps, rep from * around, ending with (2 dc, ch 2, 2 dc) in last ch-6 sp, join with sl st in 3rd ch of beg ch-3.

Rnd 6: Ch 1, sc in each st around, working 3 sc in each ch-2 sp, join with sl st in beg sc. Fasten off.

SQUARE 4
Make 10.

Rnd 1: With snow, ch 6, sl st in first ch to form ring, ch 3, 3 dc in ring, ch 3, [4 dc in ring, ch 3] 3 times, join with sl st in 3rd ch of beg ch-3. Fasten off.

Rnd 2: Join lilac with sl st in any ch-3

sp, ch 3, 2 dc in same sp, dc in each of next 4 dc, 2 dc in next ch-3 sp, dtr into ring between 4-dc groups, *3 dc in same ch-3 sp, dc in each of next 4 dc, 2 dc in next ch-3 sp, dtr into ring between 4-dc groups, rep from * around, join with sl st in 3rd ch of beg ch-3. Fasten off.

Rnd 3: Join lavender with sl st in first st of previous rnd, ch 3, dc in same st, dc in each of next 7 dc, 2 dc in next dc, ch 3, [2 dc in next dc, dc in each of next 7 dc, 2 dc in next dc, ch 3] around, join with sl st in 3rd ch of beg ch-3. Fasten off.

Rnd 4: Join snow with sl st in ch-3 sp, ch 3, dc in same ch-3 sp, dc in each of next 11 dc, 2 dc in next ch-3 sp, dtr around front post (see Stitch Guide) of dtr directly below, *2 dc in same ch-3 sp, dc in each of next 11 dc, 2 dc in next ch-3 sp, dtr around front post of dtr directly below, rep from * around, join with sl st in 3rd ch of beg ch-3. Fasten off.

Rnd 5: Join lilac with sl st in first st, ch 1, sc in each st around, working 3 sc in each dtr, join with sl st in beg sc. Fasten off.

Square 4

SQUARE 5
Make 5.

Rnd 1: With snow, ch 5, sl st in first ch to form ring, ch 1, 12 sc in ring, join with sl st in beg sc.

Rnd 2: [Ch 11, sl st in next sc] around.

Rnd 3: Sl st in each of first 6 chs, ch 1, sc in same ch *ch 3, sc in center of next ch sp, ch 3, (cl—see Special Stitches, ch 3, cl) in same ch sp, ch 3, sc in center of next ch lp, rep from * around, join in beg sc.

Square 5

Rnd 4: Sl st into ch-3 sp, ch 3, cl in same ch-3 sp, *ch 3, sc in next ch-3 sp, ch 3, (cl, ch 3, cl) in corner ch-3 sp, ch 3, sc in next ch-3 sp, ch 3, cl in next ch-3 sp, rep from * around, ending last rep with ch 3, join with sl st in 3rd ch of beg ch-3. Fasten off.

Rnd 5: Join lilac with sl st in first cl of previous rnd, ch 1, sc in top of cl, work 2 sc in each ch-3 sp, sc in each sc and in each cl with 3 sc in each corner ch-3 sp, join with sl st in beg sc. Fasten off.

SQUARE 6
Make 5.

Rnd 1: With lilac, ch 10, sl st in first ch to form ring, ch 3, 4 dc in ring, ch 7, [5 dc in ring, ch 7] 3 times, join with sl st in 3rd ch of beg ch-3.

Rnd 2: Ch 3, dc in next dc, (dc, ch 2, dc) in next dc, dc in each of next 2 dc, ch 2, (3 dc, ch 5, 3 dc) in corner ch-7 sp, ch 2, *dc in each of next 2 dc, (dc, ch 2, dc) in next dc, dc in each of next 2 dc, ch 2, (3 dc, ch 5, 3 dc) in corner

Square 6

ch-7 sp, ch 2, rep from * around, join with sl st in 3rd ch of ch-3.

Rnd 3: Ch 2, **dc dec** (see Stitch Guide) in next 5 sts, ch 5, sk next dc, dc in next dc, ch 3, (2 dc, ch 2, 2 dc) in next ch-5 sp, ch 3, sk next dc, dc in next dc, ch 5, *[dc dec in next 6 sts, ch 5, sk next dc, dc in next dc, ch 3, (2 dc, ch 2, 2 dc) in next ch-5 sp, ch 3, sk next dc, dc in next dc, ch 5, rep from * around, join in 2nd ch of beg ch-2.

Rnd 4: Ch 1, 3 sc in each ch-3 sp, sc in each dc and 2 sc in each corner ch-2 sp around, join with sl st in beg sc. Fasten off.

SQUARE 7
Make 3.

Rnd 1: With lilac, ch 6, sl st in first ch to form ring, ch 3, dc in ring, [ch 3, 3 dc in ring] 3 times, ch 3, dc in ring, join with sl st in 3rd ch of beg ch-3.

Rnd 2: Ch 3, **pc** (see Special Stitches) in next dc, 5 dc in next ch-3 sp, pc in next dc, *dc in next dc, pc in next dc, 5 dc in next ch-3 sp, pc in next dc, rep from * around, join with sl st in 3rd ch of beg ch-3.

Rnd 3: Ch 5, sk next pc, pc in next dc, dc in next dc, 3 dc in next dc, dc in next dc, pc in next dc, ch 2, sk next pc, *dc in next dc, ch 2, sk next pc, pc in next dc, dc in next dc, 3 dc in next dc, dc in next dc, pc in next dc, ch 2, sk next pc, rep from * around, join with sl st in 3rd ch of beg ch-5.

Rnd 4: Sl st into ch-2 sp, ch 5, sk next pc, pc in next dc, dc in next dc, 3 dc in next dc, dc in next dc, pc in next

Square 7

dc, ch 2, sk next pc, dc in next ch-2 sp, ch 2, *dc in next ch-2 sp, ch 2, sk next pc, pc in next dc, dc in next dc, 3 dc in next dc, dc in next dc, pc in next dc, ch 2, sk next pc, dc in next ch-2 sp, ch 2, rep from * around, join with sl st in 3rd ch of beg ch-5.

Rnd 5: Sl st into next ch-2 sp, ch 5, *sk next pc, pc in next dc, dc in next dc, 3 dc in next dc, dc in next dc, pc in next dc, ch 2, [dc in next ch-2 sp, ch 2] 3 times, rep from * around, ending last rep with, ch 2, (dc in next ch-2 sp, ch 2) twice, join with sl st in 3rd ch of ch-5.

Rnd 6: Ch 1, sc in each dc, 2 sc in each ch-2 sp and 3 sc in each center corner dc around, join with sl st in beg sc. Fasten off.

SQUARE 8
Make 3.

Rnd 1: With lilac, ch 8, sl st in first ch to form ring, ch 3, 15 dc in ring, join with sl st in 3rd ch of beg ch-3.

Rnd 2: Ch 3, dc in same st, 2 dc in each dc around, join with sl st in 3rd ch of beg ch-3.

Rnd 3: Ch 3, pc in next dc, [dc in next dc, pc in next dc] around, join with sl st in 3rd ch of beg ch-3.

Rnd 4: Ch 1, sc in first dc, ch 2, sk next pc, [sc in next dc, ch 2, sk next pc] around, join with sl st in beg sc.

Rnd 5: Ch 3, 2 dc in next ch-2 sp, 3 dc in each of next 2 ch-2 sps, *(3 dc, ch 2, 3 dc) in next ch-2 sp, 3 dc in each of next 3 ch-2 sps, rep from * around, join with sl st in 3rd ch of ch-3.

Rnd 6: Ch 1, sc in each dc around, with 3 sc in each corner ch-2 sp, join with sl st in beg sc. Fasten off.

Square 8

ASSEMBLY
Using assembly diagram as a guide, working with lilac, sew Squares tog working in **back lps** (see Stitch Guide) only.

BOTTOM BORDER
Rnd 1: With size D hook, working in back lps only, join lilac at back bottom center corner st, ch 1, 3 sc in same st, evenly sp 18 sc across each square around bottom edge and 3 sc in each center corner st, join with sl st in first sc.

Rnd 2: Ch 3, dc in each sc around, with (dc, ch 2, dc) in each center corner sc, join in 3rd ch of ch-3.

Rnds 3 & 4: Ch 3, dc in each dc around, with (dc, ch 2, dc) in each corner ch-2 sp, join in 3rd ch of ch-3.

Reverse Single Crochet

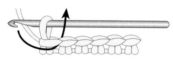

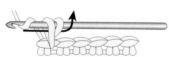

Rnd 5: Working in back lps only, sc in each st around, with sc in each ch of each corner ch-2 sp, join with sl st in beg sc.

Rnd 6: Ch 1, working from left to right, **reverse sc** (see illustration) in each sc around, join with sl st in beg sc. Fasten off.

NECKLINE BORDER
Rnd 1: With size D hook, working in back lps only, join lilac with sl st at back neck, ch 1, evenly sp 18 sc across each Square, with **sc dec** (see Stitch Guide) in center front and center back of neckline to form V-shape, join with sl st in beg sc.

Rnd 2: Ch 3, dc in each st around, working dc dec in 2 center sts at each front and back of neckline to form V-shape, join with sl st in 3rd ch of beg ch-3.

Rnd 3: Working in back lps, ch 1, sc in each st around, sc dec in 2 center front and 2 center back sts, join with sl st in beg sc.

Rnd 4: Ch 1, working from left to right, reverse sc in each sc around, join with sl st in beg sc. Fasten off. ❑❑

7 Solid Lilac	4 Tricolor	8 Solid Lilac	5 White	3 Solid Lilac	3 Lavender print Center	7 Solid Lilac	1 Lilac Center
3 Lavender print Center	1 Lilac Center	Lavender print 2 Lilac Center	4 Tricolor	White 2 Lilac Center	4 Tricolor	Lavender print 2 Lilac Center	White 2 Lilac Center
White 2 Lilac Center	2 Solid Lilac	5 White	6 Solid Lilac	1 Lilac Center	3 Solid Lilac	3 Lavender print Center	6 Solid Lilac
3 Solid Lilac	1 Lilac Center	6 Solid Lilac	NECK OPENING		5 White	1 Lilac Center	4 Tricolor
4 Tricolor	5 White	4 Tricolor			Lavender print 2 Lilac Center	8 Solid Lilac	5 White
1 White Center	8 Solid Lilac	1 White Center	2 Solid Lilac	3 Lavender print Center	3 Solid Lilac	4 Tricolor	2 Solid Lilac
White 2 Lilac Center	4 Tricolor	1 Lilac Center	4 Tricolor	1 Lilac Center	1 White Center	1 Lilac Center	Lavender print 2 Lilac Center
1 White Center	7 Solid Lilac	3 Lavender print Center	6 Solid Lilac	White 2 Lilac Center	3 Solid Lilac	4 Tricolor	6 Solid Lilac

Lavender Dreams Poncho Diagram

CROCHET

Fast & Fun

Design by Darla Sims

SKILL LEVEL
■■■☐ INTERMEDIATE

FINISHED SIZE
One size fits most young teens

MATERIALS
- ❑ Lion Brand Micro-Spun fine (sport) weight yarn (2.5 oz/168 yds/70g per skein):
    5 skeins #146 fuchsia
    5 skeins #144 lilac
    2 skeins #100 lily white
- ❑ Sizes H/8/5mm and I/9/5.5mm crochet hooks or sizes needed to obtain gauge
- ❑ Tapestry needle

GAUGE
Size H hook: 7 dc = 2 inches
Size I hook: Rnds 1–3 of Motif = 4½ inches
Take time to check gauge.

INSTRUCTIONS
PONCHO
MOTIF
Make 12 each lilac and fuchsia.
Rnd 1: With size I hook, ch 6, sl st in first ch to form ring, ch 3 *(counts as first dc throughout)*, 15 dc in ring, join with sl st in 3rd ch of beg ch-3. *(16 dc)*
Rnd 2: Ch 5 *(counts as first dc and ch 2)*, [dc in next st, ch 2] around, join with sl st in 3rd ch of beg ch-5.
Rnd 3: Sl st in first ch sp, ch 3, 2 dc

in same ch sp, ch 1, [3 dc in next ch sp, ch 1] around, join with sl st in 3rd ch of beg ch-3. *(16 3-dc groups, 16 ch-1 sps)*
Rnd 4: Sl st in each of next 2 sts, sl st in next ch sp, ch 1, sc in same ch sp, *ch 6, [sc in next ch sp, ch 3] 3 times**, sc in next ch sp, rep from * around, ending last rep at **, join with sl st in beg sc. *(12 ch-3 sps, 4 ch-6 sps)*
Rnd 5: Sl st in first ch sp, ch 3, (4 dc, ch 2, 5 dc) in same ch sp, 3 dc in each of next 3 ch sps, *(5 dc, ch 2, 5 dc) in next ch sp, 3 dc in each of next 3 ch sps, rep from * around, join with sl st in 3rd ch of beg ch-3. Fasten off. *(76 dc, 4 ch-2 sps)*
Rnd 6: With size H hook, join lily white

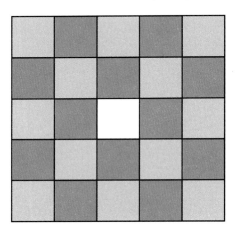

■ Fuchsia
■ Lilac
☐ Neck opening

with sc in any corner ch sp, 2 sc in same ch sp, sc in each st around with 3 sc in each corner ch sp, join with sl st in beg sc. Fasten off. *(88 sc)*
Holding Motifs WS tog, matching sts, with lily white, sew Motifs tog through **back lps** *(see Stitch Guide)* according to assembly illustration.

NECK EDGING
Rnd 1: Working around neck opening, with size H hook, join lily white with sc in any st, sc in each st around with **sc dec** *(see Stitch Guide)* in next st, in seam and in next st, join with sl st in beg sc.
Rnd 2: Ch 3, dc in each st around with **dc dec** *(see Stitch Guide)* in 3 inside corner sts, join with sl st in 3rd ch of beg ch-3.
Rnd 3: Ch 1, sc in each st around with sc dec in 3 inside corner sts, join with sl st in beg sc. Fasten off.

BOTTOM EDGING
Rnd 1: Working around bottom opening, with size H hook, join lily white with sc in any st, sc in each st and in each seam around with 3 sc in each center corner st, join with sl st in beg sc.
Rnd 2: Ch 3, dc in each st around with 3 dc in each center corner st, join with sl st in 3rd ch of beg ch-3.
Rnd 3: Ch 1, sc in each st around with 3 sc in each center corner st, join with sl st in beg sc. Fasten off.❑❑

Little Darling

Design by Brenda Reiter

FINISHED SIZES

Instructions are for girls' sizes 6–6X (small), changes for 8–10 (medium) and 12–14 (large) are in [ ]

FINISHED GARMENT MEASUREMENT

Length from top neckline ribbing to corner of granny square is 21 [23, 25] inches

MATERIALS

❏ Medium (worsted) weight yarn:
5 [6, 7] oz/250 [300, 350] yds/142 [170, 198]g light celery green
5 [6, 8] oz/250 [300, 400] yds/142 [170, 227]g blue
5 [5, 6] oz/250 [250, 300] yds/142 [142, 170]g variegated greens and blue
4 (5, 6) oz/200 [250, 300] yds/113 [142, 170]g medium sage green
❏ Size H/8/5mm crochet hook or size needed to obtain gauge
❏ Tapestry needle

GAUGE

4 dc rnds = 2 inches
Take time to check gauge.

PATTERN NOTES

Choose desired 4 yarn colors that complement one another.

Poncho is designed in 3 sizes. If only 1 number appears in pattern, it applies to all 3 sizes.

SPECIAL STITCHES

Front post double crochet (fpdc): Work dc around front post (see Stitch Guide) of stitch.

Back post double crochet (bpdc): Work dc around back post (see Stitch Guide) of stitch.

INSTRUCTIONS

PONCHO

GRANNY SQUARES

Make 24 [28, 32].

Rnd 1: With light celery green, ch 4, 2 dc in 4th ch from hook (first 3 chs count as first dc), [ch 2, 3 dc in same ch] 3 times, ch 2, join with sl st in 4th ch of beg ch-4. Fasten off. (12 dc, 4 ch-2 sps)

Rnd 2: Join medium sage green with sl st in any corner ch-2 sp, ch 3 (counts as first dc throughout), (2 dc, ch 2, 3 dc) in same ch sp, ch 1, [(3 dc, ch 2, 3 dc) in next ch-2 sp, ch 1] 3 times, join with sl st in 3rd ch of beg ch-3. Fasten off.

Rnd 3: Join blue with sl st in any corner ch-2 sp, ch 3, (2 dc, ch 2, 3 dc) in same corner ch-2 sp, *ch 1, 3 dc in next ch-1 sp, ch 1**, (3 dc, ch 2, 3 dc) in next corner ch-2 sp, rep from * around, ending last rep at **, join with sl st in 3rd ch of beg ch-3. Fasten off.

Rnd 4: Join variegated green with sl st in any corner ch-2 sp, ch 3, (2 dc, ch 2, 3 dc) in same corner ch-2 sp, *[ch 1, 3 dc in next ch-1 sp] twice, ch 1**, (3 dc, ch 2, 3 dc) in next corner ch-2 sp, rep from * around, ending last rep at **, join with sl st in 3rd ch of beg ch-3. Fasten off.

NECKLINE RIBBING

Rnd 1: With variegated green, ch 68, sl st in first ch to form ring, ch 3, working in **back bar of ch** (see illustration), dc in each ch around, join with sl st in 3rd ch of beg ch-3. (68 dc)

Back Bar of Ch

Rnd 2: Ch 2 (counts as first dc for ribbing only), **fpdc** (see Special Stitches) around next dc, [**bpdc** (see Special Stitches) around next st, fpdc around next dc] around, join with sl st in 2nd ch of beg ch-2.

Rnds 3–5: Ch 2, [fpdc around each fpdc, bpdc around each bpdc] around, join with sl st in 2nd ch of beg ch-2.

BODY

Rnd 6: Ch 3, 2 dc in same st, [ch 1, sk next 3 sts, 3 dc in next st] twice, *ch 2, 3 dc in next st, [ch 1, sk next 3 sts, 3 dc in next st] 4 times, rep from * twice, ch 2, 3 dc in next st, ch 1, sk next 3 sts, 3 dc in next st, ch 1, join with sl st in 3rd ch of beg ch-3. (5 groups of 3-dc between each corner ch-2 sp)

Rnds 7–9 [7–10, 7–11]: Sl st across sts and into next ch-1 sp, ch 3, 2 dc in same ch-1 sp, ch 1, *[3 dc in next ch-1 sp, ch 1] across to corner ch-2 sp, (3 dc, ch 2, 3 dc) in corner ch-2 sp, ch 1, rep from * around, join with sl st in 3rd ch of beg ch-3. At the end of last rnd, fasten off.

Rnd 10 [11, 12]: Join light celery with sl st in last ch-1 sp, ch 3, 2 dc in same ch-1 sp, ch 1, *[3 dc in next ch-1 sp, ch 1] across to corner ch-2 sp, (3 dc, ch 2, 3 dc) in corner ch-2 sp, ch 1, rep from * around, join with sl st in 3rd ch of beg ch-3.

Rnds 11–13 [12–15, 13–17]: Sl st into next ch-1 sp, ch 3, 2 dc in same ch-1 sp, ch 1, *[3 dc in next ch-1 sp, ch 1] across to corner ch-2 sp, (3 dc, ch 2, 3 dc) in corner ch-2 sp, ch 1, rep from * around, join with sl st in 3rd ch of beg ch-3. At the end of last rnd, fasten off.

Rnds 14–17 [16–20, 18–23]: With medium sage green, rep rnds 10–13 [11–15, 12–17].

Rnds 18–21 [21–25, 24–29]: With blue, rep rnds 10–13 [11–15, 12–17]. At end of last row, fasten off.

ASSEMBLY

Working through **back lps** (see Stitch Guide) only, place 2 Squares tog, sew across 1 side of Squares. Rep sewing Squares tog until 2 strips of 5 [6, 7] Squares are sewn tog. In same manner, sew 2 strips tog of 7 [8, 9] Squares. Sew the 2 shorter strips of

Squares to opposite ends of Poncho Body along bottom edge. Sew the rem 2 strips of Squares to the rem side of Poncho bottom.

RUFFLED TRIM
With RS facing, working in back lps only, join light celery green at bottom edge of Poncho in edge of any Square, ch 1, sc in same st, ch 5, [sc in next st, ch 5] around, join with sl st in beg sc. Fasten off.❑❑

Evening Jewel

Design by Tammy Hildebrand

SKILL LEVEL
 EASY

FINISHED SIZE
One size fits most (41 inches square)

MATERIALS
- Lion Brand Homespun bulky (chunky) weight yarn:
    19 oz/585 yds/538g #305 modern (blue/green ombre)
- Lion Brand Fun Fur fine (sport) weight novelty eyelash yarn:
    2 oz/69 yds/57g #170 peacock
- Size P/15mm crochet hook or size needed to obtain gauge

GAUGE
2 strands bulky yarn held tog as 1:
2 2-dc groups = 3 inches; 1 dc row
= 1¼ inches
Take time to check gauge.

PATTERN NOTES
Work with 2 strands bulky yarn held together as 1 throughout.

Beginning chain-3 counts as first double crochet.

Join with a slip stitch unless otherwise stated.

SPECIAL STITCH
V-stitch (V-st): (Dc, ch 2, dc) in next st or ch sp.

PONCHO
Rnd 1: With 2 strands bulky yarn held tog as one, ch 40, join in first ch to from ring, ch 3, dc in each of next 8 chs, **V-st** (see Special Stitch) in next ch, [dc in each of next 9 chs, V-st in next ch] around, join in 3rd ch of beg ch-3. (36 dc, 4 V-sts)

Rnd 2: Ch 1, sc in first st, ch 3, sk next st, [sc in next st, ch 3, sk next st] 4 times, (sc, ch 2, sc) in next ch sp, [ch 3, sk next st, {sc in next st, ch 3, sk next st} 5 times, (sc, ch 2, sc) in next ch sp] 3 times, ch 3, sk last st, join in beg sc. (28 sc, 24 ch-3 sps, 4 ch-2 sps)

Rnd 3: Sl st in next ch sp, (ch 3, dc) in same sp, 2 dc in each ch-3 sp around with V-st in each ch-2 sp, join in 3rd ch of beg ch-3. (48 dc, 4 V-sts)

Rnd 4: Sl st back into sp between last 2-dc group and ch-3, ch 1, sc in same sp, *[ch 3, sc in sp between next 2-dc groups] across to next V-st, ch 3, dc in sp between 2-dc group and V-st, ch 3, (sc, ch 2, sc) in ch sp of next V-st, ch 3, sc in sp between same V-st and next 2-dc group; rep from * 3 times, ch 3, join in beg sc. *(32 ch-3 sps, 4 ch-2 sps)*

Rnd 5: Rep rnd 3. *(64 dc, 4 V-sts)*

Rnd 6: Sl st back into sp between last 2-dc group and ch-3, ch 1, sc in same sp, *[ch 3, sc in sp between next 2-dc groups] across to next V-st, ch 3, dc in sp between 2-dc group and V-st, ch 3, (sc, ch 2, sc) in ch sp of next V-st, ch 3, sc in sp between same V-st and next 2-dc group; rep from * 3 times, [ch 3, sc in sp between next 2-dc groups] across, ch 3, join in beg sc. *(40 ch-3 sps, 4 ch-2 sps)*

Rnds 7–20 or to desired length: Rep rnds 3 and 6 alternately. Fasten off at end of last rnd.

BOTTOM TRIM

Rnd 1: Join 1 strand eyelash in any ch sp on last rnd of Poncho, ch 3, 4 dc in same sp, 5 dc in each ch sp around, join in 3rd ch of beg ch-3. Fasten off.

Rnd 2: Working around posts of sts on last rnd of Poncho, join 1 strand eyelash around any st, ch 3, 4 dc around post of same st, 5 dc around post of each st around, join in 3rd ch of beg ch-3. Fasten off.

NECK TRIM

Rnd 1: Working in starting ch on opposite side of rnd 1 on Poncho, join 1 strand eyelash in any ch, ch 3, 2 dc in same ch, 3 dc in each ch around. Fasten off.

Rnd 2: Working around post of sts on rnd 1 of Poncho, join 1 strand eyelash around any st, ch 3, 2 dc around post of same st, 3 dc around post of each st around, join in 3rd ch of beg ch-3. Fasten off.❑❑

CROCHET

Monoghan

Design by Joyce Nordstrom

SKILL LEVEL
■■■■▬ EXPERIENCED

FINISHED SIZES
Instructions are given for small/medium sizes, changes for large/x-large are in [ ]

MATERIALS
❑ Medium (worsted) weight yarn: 12 [14] oz/600 [700] yds/340 [397]g each gray and white

❑ Size K/10½/6.5mm double-ended crochet hook or size needed to obtain gauge
❑ Size I/9/5.5mm crochet hook
❑ Tapestry needle
❑ Stitch markers

GAUGE
Double-ended hook: 7 sts = 2 inches, 12 pattern rows = 2¾ inches
Take time to check gauge.

PATTERN NOTES
To **pull up lp**, insert hook in vertical bar, yo, pull lp through leaving lp on hook.

When **picking up lps,** leave all lps on hook unless otherwise stated.

To **turn,** rotate hook 180 degrees and slide all lps to opposite end. Do not turn unless otherwise stated.

To **work lps off hook when adding a new color,** with new color, place slip knot on hook, pull slip knot through first lp on hook, [yo, pull through 2 lps on hook] across.

To **work lps off with color already in use,** pick up color from row below, yo, pull through 1 lp on hook, [yo, pull through 2 lps on hook] across. You will always have 1 lp left on your hook at the end after working lps off; this will be the first st of the next row.

SPECIAL STITCHES
Single crochet loop (sc lp): Pull up lp in specified bar or st, yo, pull through 1 lp on hook.

Treble loop (tr lp): Yo 2 times, insert hook in specified st or bar, yo, pull lp through, [yo, pull through 2 lps on hook] twice. Sk next vertical bar on last row behind tr lp.

Double treble crochet front post lp (dtr fp lp): Yo 3 times, insert hook from front to back around post of specified st, yo, pull lp through, [yo, pull through 2 lps on hook] 3 times. Sk next vertical bar on last row behind dtr fp lp.

Gray cable: Sk first post st of next 2 post st group, dtr fp lp around next post st, pull up lp in each of next 2 vertical bars on last row, dtr fp lp around skipped post st.

White cable: Sk first post st of next 2 post st group, dtr fp lp around next post st, sc lp in each of next 2 vertical bars on last row, dtr fp lp around sk post st.

Double treble crochet front post (dtr fp): Yo 3 times, insert hook from front to back around post of specified st, yo, pull lp through, [yo, pull through 2 lps on hook] 4 times. Sk next vertical bar on last row behind post st.

INSTRUCTIONS
PONCHO
PANEL
Make 2.

Row 1: With double-ended hook and gray, ch 78, pull up lp in 2nd ch from hook *(see Pattern Notes)*, pull up lp in each ch across, turn. *(78 lps on hook)*

Row 2: With white, work lps off hook, **do not turn.**

Row 3: Ch 1, sk first vertical bar, **sc lp** *(see Special Stitches)* in each vertical bar across, turn.

Row 4: With gray, work lps off hook, **do not turn.**

Row 5: Ch 1, sk first vertical bar, pull up lp in each of next 9 vertical

bars, *tr lp (see Special Stitches) in corresponding st on row 2, pull up lp in each of next 2 vertical bars on last row, sk next 2 sts on row 2, tr lp in next st, pull up lp in each of next 4 vertical bars on last row, tr lp in corresponding st on row 2, pull up lp in each of next 2 vertical bars on last row, sk next 2 sts on row 2, tr lp in next st*, pull up lp in each of next 34 vertical bars on last row, rep between *, pull up lp in each of last 10 vertical bars on last row, turn.

Row 6: With white, work lps off hook, **do not turn.**

Row 7: Ch 1, sk first vertical bar, sc lp in each of next 9 vertical bars, *tr lp in vertical bar of corresponding st 4 rows below, sc lp in each of next 2 vertical bars on last row, sk next 2 sts 4 rows below, tr lp in vertical bar of next st, sc lp in each of next 4 vertical bars on last row, tr lp in vertical bar of corresponding st 4 rows below, sc lp in each of next 2 vertical bars of last row, sk next 2 sts 4 rows below, tr lp in next st*, sc lp in each of next 34 vertical bars on last row, rep between *, sc lp in each of last 10 vertical bars on last row, turn.

Row 8: With gray, work lps off hook, **do not turn.**

Row 9: Ch 1, sk first vertical bar, pull up lp in each of next 9 vertical bars, *work **gray cable** (see Special Stitches), pull up lp in each of next 4 vertical bars, work gray cable*, pull up lp in each of next 34 vertical bars, rep between *, pull up lp in each of last 10 vertical bars, turn.

Row 10: With white, work lps off hook, **do not turn.**

Row 11: Ch 1, sk first vertical bar, sc lp in each of next 9 vertical bars, *work **white cable** (see Special Stitches), sc lp in each of next 4 vertical bars, work white cable*, sc lp in each of next 34 vertical bars, rep between *, sc lp in each of last 10 vertical bars, turn.

Row 12: With gray, work lps off hook, **do not turn.**

Row 13: Ch 1, sk first vertical bar, pull up lp in each of next 9 vertical bars, *tr lp around post of first st of next 2-post st group, pull up lp in each of next 2 vertical bars on last row, tr lp around post of next st of same group, pull up lp in each of next 4 vertical bars on last row, tr lp around post of first st of next 2-post st group, pull up lp in each of next 2 vertical bars on last row, tr lp around post of next st of same group*, pull up lp in each of next 34 vertical bars on last row, rep between *, pull up lp in each of last 10 vertical bars on last row, turn.

Row 14: With white, work lps off hook, **do not turn.**

Row 15: Ch 1, sk first vertical bar, sc lp in each of next 9 vertical bars, *tr lp around post of first st of next 2-post st group, sc lp in each of next 2 vertical bars on last row, tr lp around post of next st of same group, sc lp in each of next 4 vertical bars on last row, tr lp around post of first st of next 2-post st group, sc lp in each of next 2 vertical bars on last row, tr lp around post of next st of same group*, sc lp in each of next 34 vertical bars on last row, rep between *, sc lp in each of last 10 vertical bars on last row, turn.

Rows 16–122 [16–130]: Rep rows 8–15 consecutively, ending with row 10.

Row 123 [131]: Sl st in each of first 10 vertical bars, ***dtr fp** (see Special Stitches) around post of 2nd st of next 2-post st group, sl st in each of next 2 vertical bars on last row, dtr fp around post of first st of same group, sl st in each of next 4 vertical bars on last row, dtr fp around post of 2nd st of next 2-post st group, sl st in each of next 2 vertical bars on last row, dtr fp around post of first st of same group*, sl st in each of next 34 vertical bars on last row, rep between *, sl st in each of last 10 vertical bars on last row. Fasten off.

ASSEMBLY

With predominantly gray side of Panels facing, place stitch marker 7 [8½] inches below upper right corner on each Panel. Place end of 2nd Panel against side of first Panel, (see letters A on assembly illustration). Working through both thicknesses and easing to fit, with size I hook and gray, join with sc in first st to the left, working from left to right, [ch 1, sk next st, **reverse sc** (see illustration) in next st] across. Fasten off.

Reverse Single Crochet

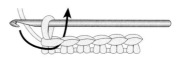
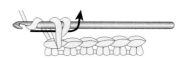

Place end of first Panel against side of 2nd Panel (see letters B on assembly illustration), join in same manner stopping at marker. **Do not fasten off.** Working in sts and in ends of rows around neck opening, evenly sp sts so piece lies flat, [ch 1, sk next st or row, reverse sc in next st or row] around, sl st in seam. Fasten off.❑❑

Assembly Illustration

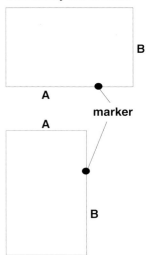

Honeycomb Lace

Design by George Shaheen

SKILL LEVEL
■■□□ EASY

FINISHED SIZES
Woman's small/medium (large/ extra-large) Instructions are given for smallest size, with larger sizes in parentheses. When only 1 number is given, it applies to all sizes.

MATERIALS
❑ Wool-Ease Sportweight 80 percent acrylic/ 20 percent wool fine (sport) weight yarn from Lion Brand (5 oz/435 yds per skein): 1 skein fisherman #099
❑ Size 8 (5mm) needles or size needed to obtain gauge

GAUGE
20 sts = 4 inches/10cm in pat st
To save time, take time to check gauge.

SPECIAL ABBREVIATION
C4B (CABLE 4 BACK): Sl 2 sts onto cn, hold in back; k2; k2 from cn

PANEL
Make 2.
Cast on 51 sts.
Row 1 (WS): K1, p4, k46.
Row 2 (RS): K45, p1, C4B, p1.
Row 3: K1, p4, k1, *k2tog, [yo] twice, k2tog; rep from * to last st, k1.
Row 4: K2, [work (k1, p1) in double yo, k2] 10 times, (k1, p1) in double yo, k1, p1, k4, p1.
Row 5: K1, p4, k1, *yo, [k2tog] twice, yo; rep from * to last st, k1.
Row 6: K4, [work (k1, p1) in double yo, k2] 10 times, k1, p1, C4B, p1.
Rep Rows 3–6 until panel measures approx 20 (21½) inches, ending with Row 6 of pat.
Next row: K1, p4, k46.
Bind off as follows: K45, k2tog, k1, k2tog, k1.

ASSEMBLY
Block pieces to measure 20½ (22) x 9 inches.

Referring to Fig. 1, sew pieces tog with cable edge at neckline.

FRINGE
Cut strands of yarn, each 4 inches long.
Holding 4 strands tog, fold each group in half.
Working along 1 edge, insert crochet hook from WS to RS. Pull fold of fringe through fabric. Draw ends through loop and fasten tightly.
Tie knots through every other st across cast-on edges, through each yo across side edges, and at each V.
Trim fringe evenly.❑❑

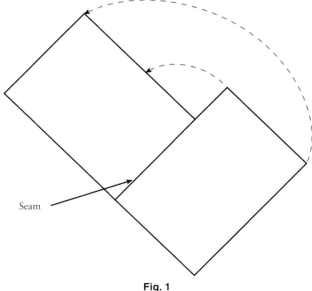

Seam

Fig. 1

Ultra Fun

Design by Melissa Leapman

SKILL LEVEL
■■■□ INTERMEDIATE

FINISHED SIZE
One size fits most

FINISHED MEASUREMENTS
Approx 56 inches wide x 15 inches long

MATERIALS
- ❏ Wool-Ease® Thick and Quick 80 percent acrylic/20 percent wool bulky weight yarn from Lion Brand (6 oz/108 yds per skein): 6 skeins sky blue #106

  5 BULKY
- ❏ Size 13 (9mm) 39-inch circular needle or size needed to obtain gauge
- ❏ Stitch markers
- ❏ Size H/8 (5mm) crochet hook

GAUGE
10 sts and 14 rows = 4 inches/10cm in in St st
To save time, take time to check gauge.

SPECIAL ABBREVATIONS
(M1) Make One: Insert LH needle from front to back under horizontal bar between sts, knit into the back of this lp.
Sm: Slip marker.

PATTERN NOTE
Poncho is worked in rounds and 1 piece from neck downward.

PONCHO
Cast on 56 sts. Join without twisting, pm between first and last st.
Ribbing Rnd: *K1, p1; rep from * around.
Rep Ribbing rnd until ribbing measures 9 inches from cast-on edge.

Shape shoulders
Rnd 1: K26 for back, pm, k2 for side seam, pm, k26 for front, pm, k2 for side seam, pm.
Rnd 2: Knit to first marker, M1, sm,

k2, sm, M1, knit to next marker, M1, sm, k2, sm, M1–60 sts.
[Rep Rnd 2] 10 times–100 sts.

Beg body
On following rnds, slip markers as you come to them.
Rnd 1: Knit.
Rnd 2: K48, M1, k2, M1, k48, M1, k2, M1–104 sts.
Rnd 3: Knit.
Inc rnd: Knit to first marker, M1, k2, M1, knit to next marker, M1, k2, M1–108 sts.
Rnds 5–8: Rep Rnds 3 and 4–116 sts.
[Knit 3 rnds, rep inc rnd] 6 times–140 sts.
Knit 3 rnds.

Remove all but end of rnd markers.
Purl 1 rnd.
Next rnd: *K2tog, yo, k5; rep from * around.
Purl 1 rnd.
Bind off knitwise.

FRINGE
Cut strands of yarn, each 16 inches long.
Holding 6 strands tog, fold each group in half.
Working along one edge, insert crochet hook from WS to RS in yo space at lower edge of poncho. Pull fold of fringe through fabric. Draw ends through loop and fasten tightly.
Rep in each yo space.
Trim fringe evenly.❏❏

Jewels & Lace

Design by Darla Sims

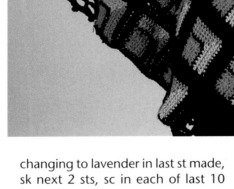

SKILL LEVEL
■■□□ EASY

FINISHED SIZE
36 inches wide x 36 inches long
One size fits most.

MATERIALS
❑ Lion Brand Micro-Spun
  fine (sport) weight yarn
  (2.5 oz/168 yds/70g
  per skein):
  - 13 skeins #153 black
  - 2 skeins #146 fuchsia
  - 2 skeins #143 lavender
  - 2 skeins #144 lilac
❑ Sizes G/6/4mm and H/8/5mm
  crochet hooks or size needed to
  obtain gauge
❑ Tapestry needle

GAUGE
Size H hook: 4 sc = 1 inch; 4 sc rows
= 1 inch
Take time to check gauge.

PATTERN NOTES
Beginning chain-3 counts as first double
  crochet.
Join with slip stitch unless otherwise
  stated
When **changing colors** (see Stitch Guide),
  always drop yarn to wrong side of work.
  Use a separate ball of yarn for each color
  section. Do not carry yarn across from
  one section to another. Fasten off colors
  at end of each color section.

SPECIAL STITCH
Picot: Ch 3, sl st in 3rd ch from hook.

SQUARE
Make 94.
Row 1 (RS): With size H hook and black,
ch 27, sc in 2nd ch from hook and in
each of next 11 chs, sk next 2 chs, sc
in each of last 12 chs, turn. (24 sc)
Row 2: Ch 1, sc in each of first 11 sts,
sk next 2 sts, sc in each of last 11 sts
changing color (see Pattern Notes)
to lilac in last st made, turn. (22 sc)
Row 3: Ch 1, sc in each of first 10 sts,

changing to lavender in last st made,
sk next 2 sts, sc in each of last 10
sts, turn. (20 sc)
Row 4: Ch 1, sc in each of first 9 sts,
changing to lilac in last st made, sk
next 2 sts, sc in each of last 9 sts,
turn. (18 sc)
Row 5: Ch 1, sc in each of first 8 sts,
changing to lavender in last st made,
sk next 2 sts, sc in each of last 8 sts,
turn. (16 sc)
Row 6: Ch 1, sc in each of first 7 sts,
changing to lilac in last st made, sk next
2 sts, sc in each of last 7 sts, changing

to black in last st made, turn. (14 sc)
Row 7: Ch 1, sc in each of first 6 sts,
sk next 2 sts, sc in each of last 6 sts,
changing to fuchsia in last st made,
turn. (12 sc)
Row 8: Ch 1, sc in each of first 5 sts,
sk next 2 sts, sc in each of last 5 sts,
turn. (10 sc)
Row 9: Ch 1, sc in each of first 4 sts,
sk next 2 sts, sc in each of last 4 sts,
turn. (8 sc)
Row 10: Ch 1, sc in each of first 3 sts,
sk next 2 sts, sc in each of last 3 sts,
turn. (6 sc)

Row 11: Ch 1, sc in each of first 2 sts, sk next 2 sts, sc in each of last 2 sts, turn. *(4 sc)*

Row 12: Ch 1, sc in first st, sk next 2 sts, sc in last st, turn. Fasten off. *(2 sc)*

Rnd 13: Now working in rnds, with size G hook and black, join with sc in any st, sc in each st and in end of each row around with 3 sc in each corner st, join in beg sc. Fasten off.

LACE INSERT
Make 21.

Row 1 (RS): With size H hook and black, ch 4, 2 dc in 4th ch from hook, turn. *(3 dc)*

Row 2: (Ch 3, dc) in first st, 3 dc in next st, 2 dc in last st, turn. *(7 dc)*

Row 3: Ch 4 *(counts as first dc and ch-1 sp)*, dc in next st, [ch 1, dc in next st] across, turn. *(7 dc, 6 ch sps)*

Row 4: Ch 5 *(counts as first dc and ch-2 sp)*, dc in next st, [ch 2, dc in next st] across, turn.

Rows 5 & 6: Ch 6 *(counts as first dc and ch-3 sp)*, dc in next st, [ch 3, dc in next st] across, turn.

Rnd 7: Now working in rnds, with size G hook, ch 1, sc in first st, [(2 dc, **picot**—*see Special Stitch*, 2 dc) in next ch sp, dc in next st] across, 3 dc in end of each row around, join in beg sc. Fasten off.

Sew Squares and Lace Inserts tog through **back lps** *(see Stitch Guide)* according to assembly diagram.

NECK TRIM
Working between Lace Inserts on one side of neck edge, with G hook and black, join with sc in first st on Squares after Lace Insert, sc in each st across to other Lace Insert. Fasten off.

Rep on other side of neck between Lace Inserts.

PONCHO TRIM
Working on bottom edge of Poncho between ends of Lace Inserts, with G hook and black, join with sc in first st after Lace Insert, sc in each st across to opposite end of Lace Inserts with 3 sc in tip of point. Fasten off. ❏❏

Assembly Diagram

 = Lace Insert placement

CROCHET

Portadown

Design by Joyce Nordstrom

SKILL LEVEL
◼◼◼▷ EXPERIENCED

FINISHED SIZE
One size fits all

MATERIALS
❏ Medium (worsted) weight yarn: **[4] MEDIUM**
  16 oz/800 yds/454g each buff and variegated
  1 oz/50 yds/28g each navy, sage and burgundy

❏ Size K/10½/6.5mm double-end hook crochet hook or size needed to obtain gauge
❏ Size I/9/5.5mm crochet hook
❏ Tapestry needle

GAUGE
Double-end hook: 7 sts = 2 inches, 6 rows worked in pattern = 1 inch Take time to check gauge.

PATTERN NOTES
Because the double-ended crochet hook creates a smaller stitch, when working edgings, you may need to use a regular hook one size smaller than the double-ended hook.

To **pull up lp**, insert hook in vertical bar, yo, pull lp through leaving lps on hook.

When **picking up lps,** leave all lps on hook unless otherwise stated.

To **turn,** rotate hook 180 degrees and slide all lps to opposite end. Do not turn unless otherwise stated.

To **work lps off hook when adding**

a new color, with new color, place sl knot on hook, pull sp knot through first lp on hook, [yo, pull through 2 lps on hook **or,** yo 2 times with new color, insert hook around post of tr lp, yo, pull lp through, (yo, pull through 2 lps on hook) 2 times.] across.

To **change colors when working across row,** drop current color, [pull next color through 2 lps on hook, or yo twice with new color, insert hook around post of tr lp, yo, pull lp through, [yo, pull through 2 lps on hook] twice, use a separate skein or ball of yarn for each color section, do not carry yarn from one section to another. Fasten off colors at end of each color section.

To **work lps off with color already in use,** pick up color from row below, yo, pull through 1 lp on hook, [yo, pull through 2 lps on hook] across. You will always have 1 lp left on your hook at the end after working lps off, this will be the first st of the next row. If you have difficulty keeping all the stitches on the double-end hook,

cap the unused end of hook with either a knitting needle protector or a clean wine cork.

Use a separate skein or ball of yarn for each color section, do not carry yarn across from one section to another. Fasten off colors at end of each color section.

SPECIAL STITCHES

Treble loop (tr lp): Yo twice, insert hook in next vertical bar on row 4 rows below, yo, pull lp through, [yo, pull 2 lps on hook] twice. Sk next st on last row behind tr lp.

Treble loop front post (tr fp): Yo twice, insert hook from front to back around post *(see Stitch Guide)* next tr or tr fp, yo, pull lp through, (yo, pull through 2 lps on hook) twice. Sk next st on last row behind tr fp.

Treble decrease (tr dec): *Yo twice, insert hook around post of st, yo, pull lp through, [yo, pull through 2 lps on hook] twice, rep from *, yo, pull through all lps on hook.

Decrease (dec): Insert hook in next 2 vertical bars at same time, yo, pull lp through.

INSTRUCTIONS
PONCHO
FIRST SIDE

Row 1: Starting at front, with double-end hook and variegated, ch 79, pull up lp in 2nd ch from hook *(see Pattern Notes),* pull up lp in each ch across, turn. *(79 lps on hook)*

Row 2: With buff, work lps off hook, **do not turn.**

Row 3: Sk first vertical bar, pull up lp in each vertical bar across, turn.

Row 4: With variegated, work lps off hook, **do not turn.**

Row 5: Sk first vertical bar, pull up lp in each vertical bar across, turn.

Rows 6–13: Rep rows 2–5 consecutively.

Row 14: With buff, work 14 lps off hook, with sage, work 3 lps off hook, with buff, work 21 lps off hook, with burgundy, work 3 lps off hook, with buff, work 21 lps off hook, with navy, work 3 lps off hook, with buff, work 14 lps off hook, **do not turn.**

Row 15: Sk first vertical bar, pull up lp in each of next 13 vertical bars, with navy, *sk next corresponding st 4 rows below, **tr lp** *(see Special Stitches)* in next st, pull up lp in next vertical bar, tr lp in same st as last tr lp*, with buff, pull up lp in each of next 21 vertical bars on last row, with burgundy, rep between *, with buff, pull up lp in each of next 21 vertical bars, with sage, rep between *, with buff, pull up lp in each of last 14 vertical bars, turn.

Note: *Continue to work navy, burgundy and sage in established color patterns.*

Row 16: With variegated, work lps off hook, **do not turn.**

Row 17: Sk first vertical bar, pull up lp in each of next 12 vertical bars, [*sk corresponding and next st 4 rows below, tr lp around next st, with color, pull up lp in each of next 3 vertical bars on last row, with variegated, tr lp around same st as last tr lp*, pull up lp in each of 19 vertical bars] twice, rep between *, pull up lp in each of last 13 vertical bars, turn.

Row 18: With buff, work 13 lps off hook, [with color, work 5 lps off hook, with buff, work 19 lps off hook] twice, with color, work 5 lps off hook, with buff, work 13 lps off hook, **do not turn.**

Row 19: Sk first vertical bar, pull up lp in each of next 11 vertical bars, with color, ***tr fp** (see Special Stitches), pull up lp in each of next 5 vertical bars, tr fp**, with buff, pull up lp in each of next 17 vertical bars, rep from * across, ending last rep at **, pull up lp in each of last 12 vertical bars, turn.

Row 20: With variegated, work lps off hook, **do not turn.**

Row 21: Sk first vertical bar, pull up lp in each of next 10 vertical bars, *tr fp, with color, pull up lp in each of next 7 vertical bars, with variegated, tr fp**, pull up lp in each of next 15 vertical bars, rep from * across, ending last rep at **, pull up lp in each of last 11 vertical bars, turn.

Row 22: With buff, work 12 lps off hook, [with color, work 7 lps off hook, with buff, work 17 lps off hook] twice, with color, work 7 lps off hook, with buff, work 12 lps off hook, **do not turn.**

Row 23: Sk first vertical bar, pull up lp in each of next 9 vertical bars, *with color, tr fp, pull up lp in each of next 9 vertical bars, tr fp**, with buff, pull up lp in each of next 13 vertical bars, rep from * around, ending last rep at **, with buff, pull up lp in each of last 10 vertical bars, turn.

Row 24: With variegated, work lps off hook, **do not turn.**

Row 25: Sk first vertical bar, pull up lp in each of next 8 vertical bars, *tr fp, with color, pull up lp in each of next 11 vertical bars, with variegated, tr fp**, pull up lp in next 11 vertical bars, rep from * around, ending last rep at **, pull up lp in each of last 9 vertical bars, turn.

Row 26: With buff, work 10 lps off hook, [with color, work 11 lps off hook, with buff, work 13 lps off hook] twice, with color, work 11 lps off hook, with buff, work 10 lps off hook, **do not turn.**

Row 27: Sk first vertical bar, pull up lp in each of next 7 vertical bars, *with color, tr fp, pull up lp in each of next 13 vertical bars, tr fp**, with buff, pull up lp in next 9 vertical bars, rep from * across, ending last rep at **, with buff, pull up lp in each of last 8 vertical bars, turn.

Row 28: With variegated, work lps off hook, **do not turn.**

Row 29: Sk first vertical bar, pull up lp in each of next 6 vertical bars, [tr fp, with color, pull up lp in each of next 15 vertical bars, with variegated, tr fp, pull up lp in each of next 7 vertical bars] 3 times, turn.

Row 30: With buff, work 8 lps off hook, [with color, work 15 lps off hook, with buff, work 9 lps off hook] twice, with color, work 15 lps off hook, with buff, work last 8 lps off hook, **do not turn.**

Row 31: Sk first vertical bar, pull up lp in each of next 5 vertical bars, *with color, tr fp, pull up lp in each next 17 vertical bars, tr fp**, with buff, pull up lp in each of next 5 vertical bars, rep from * across, ending last rep at **, with buff, pull up lp in each of last 6 vertical bars, turn.

Row 32: With variegated, work lps off hook, **do not turn.**

Row 33: Sk first vertical bar, pull up lp in each of next 4 vertical bars, *tr fp, with color, pull up lp in each of next 19 vertical bars, with variegated, tr fp**, pull up lp in each of next 3 vertical bars, rep from * across, ending last rep at **, pull up lp in each of last 5 vertical bars, turn.

Row 34: With buff, work 7 lps off hook, [with color, work 17 lps off hook, with buff, work 5 lps off hook] twice, with color, work 17 lps off hook, with buff, work last 7 lps off hook, **do not turn.**

Rows 35 & 36: Rep rows 31 and 32.
Rows 37 & 38: Rep rows 29 and 30.
Rows 39 & 40: Rep rows 27 and 28.
Rows 41 & 42: Rep rows 25 and 26.
Rows 43 & 44: Rep rows 23 and 24.
Row 45: Rep row 21.
Row 46: With buff, work 12 lps off hook, [with color, work 7 lps off hook, with buff, work 17 lps off hook] twice, with color, work 7 lps off hook, with buff, work last 12 lps off hook, **do not turn.**

Rows 47 & 48: Rep rows 19 and 20.
Row 49: Sk first vertical bar, pull up lp in each of next 12 vertical bars, *tr fp, with color pull up lp in each of next 3 vertical bars, with variegated, tr fp**, pull up lp in each of next 19 vertical bars, rep from * across, ending last rep at **, pull up lp in each of last 13 vertical bars, turn.

Row 50: With buff, work 14 lps off hook, [with color, work 3 lps off hook, with buff, work 21 lps off hook] twice, with color, work 3 lps off hook, with buff, work last 14 lps off hook, **do not turn.**

Row 51: Sk first vertical bar, pull up lp in each of next 13 vertical bars, *with color, tr fp, pull up lp in next vertical bar, tr fp**, with buff, pull up lp in each of next 21 vertical bars, rep from * across, ending last rep at **, with buff, pull up lp in each of last 14 vertical bars, turn.

Row 52: With variegated, work lp off hook, **do not turn.**

Row 53: Sk first vertical bar, pull up lp in each of next 14 vertical bars, ***tr dec** (see Special Stitches) in next 2 post sts, sk next vertical bar**, pull up lp in each of next 23 vertical bars, rep from * across, ending last rep at **, pull up lp in each of last 15 vertical bars, turn.

Row 54: With buff, work lps off hook, **do not turn.**

Row 55: Sk first vertical bar, pull up lp in each of next 14 vertical bars, *with color, tr dec next 2 post sts, sk next vertical bar**, with buff, pull up lp in each of next 23 sts, rep from * across, ending last rep at **, with buff, pull up lp in each of last 15 vertical bars, turn.

Rows 56 & 57: Rep rows 4 and 5.
Next Rows: Rep rows 2–5 consecutively for 20 inches or to desired length, ending with row 4.

NECK

Row 1: Sk first vertical bar, pull up lp in each of next 65 vertical bars leaving remaining bars unworked for neck opening, turn. (66 lps on hook)

Row 2: With buff, work lps off hook, **do not turn.**

Row 3: Sk first 2 vertical bars, pull up lp in each vertical bar across, turn. (65 lps)

Row 4: With variegated, work lps off hook, **do not turn.**

Row 5: Sk first vertical bar, pull up lp

in each vertical bar across to last 2 bars, **dec** (*see Special Stitches*), turn. *(64 lps)*

Rows 6–9: Rep rows 2–5 ending with *(62 lps)* in last row.

Row 10: With buff, work lps off hook, **do not turn.**

Row 11: Pull up lp in first vertical bar, pull up lp in each vertical bar across, turn. *(63 lps)*

Row 12: With variegated, work lps off hook, **do not turn.**

Row 13: Sk first vertical bar, pull up lp in each vertical bar across to last bar, pull up lp in top strand of next **horizontal bar** (*see illustration*), pull up lp in last vertical bar, turn. *(64 lps)*

Horizontal Bar

Rows 14–17: Rep rows 10–13, ending with *(66 lps)* in last row.

Row 18: With buff, work lps off hook, holding buff and 1 strand variegated tog, ch 13, drop variegated, **do not turn.**

Row 19: Pull up lp in 2nd ch from hook, pull up lp in each ch across, pull up lp in each vertical bar across, turn. *(79 lps)*

Rows 20 & 21: Rep rows 4 and 5.

Next Rows: For **back,** rep rows 2–5 consecutively to desired length.

Last Row: Sk first vertical bar, sl st in each vertical bar across. Fasten off.

SECOND SIDE

Row 1: Starting at front, with double-end hook and variegated, ch 79, pull up lp in 2nd ch from hook and in each ch across, turn. *(79 lps on hook)*

Row 2: With buff, work lps off hook, **do not turn.**

Row 3: Sk first vertical bar, pull up lp in each vertical bar across, turn.

Row 4: With variegated, work lps off hook, **do not turn.**

Row 5: Rep row 3.

Next Rows: Rep rows 2–5 consecutively to desired length, ending with row 4. At end of last row, fasten off.

NECK

Row 1: For **neck opening,** sk first 13 vertical bars, join variegated with sl st in next vertical bar, pull up lp in each vertical bar across, turn. *(66 lps)*

Row 2: With buff, work lps off hook, **do not turn.**

Row 3: Sk first vertical bar, pull up lp in each vertical bar across to last 2 vertical bars, dec, turn. *(65 lps)*

Row 4: With variegated, work lps off hook, **do not turn.**

Row 5: Sk first 2 vertical bars, pull up lp in each vertical bar across, turn. *(64 lps)*

Rows 6–9: Rep rows 2–5, ending with 62 lps in last row.

Row 10: With buff, work lps off hook, **do not turn.**

Row 11: Sk first vertical bar, pull up lp in each vertical bar across to last bar, pull up lp in top strand of next horizontal bar, pull up lp in last vertical bar, turn. *(63 lps)*

Row 12: With variegated, work lps off hook, **do not turn.**

Row 13: Sk first vertical bar, pull up lp in top strand of next horizontal bar, pull up lp in each vertical bar across, turn. *(64 lps)*

Rows 14–17: Rep rows 10–13, ending with *(66 lps)* in last row. At end of last row, fasten off.

Row 18: With 1 strand buff and variegated held tog, ch 13, drop variegated, work lps off hook, **do not turn.**

Row 19: Sk first vertical bar, pull up lp in each vertical bar across, pull up lp in each ch across, turn. *(79 lps)*

Rows 20 & 21: Rep rows 4 and 5.

Next Rows: For **back,** rep rows 2–5 consecutively to desired length, ending with row 4.

Last Row: Sk first vertical bar, sl st in each vertical bar across. Fasten off.

For **center front seam,** matching ends of rows on each Side, with variegated, sew 18 inches tog starting at row 1.

For **center back seam,** sew ends of rows tog.

For **trim** on center front seam, working vertically across center front seam, with RS facing, join variegated with sc

Reverse Single Crochet

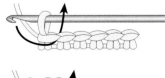

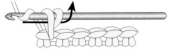

in top of seam, working from left to right, *ch 1, sk next 3 rows, **reverse sc** (*see illustration*) in next row, rep from * across. Fasten off.

Rep on back seam.

NECK BORDER

Row 1: Working in ends of rows and in sts across neck opening, join variegated with sc in first row after front seam on right-hand side, working left to right, evenly spacing sts, [ch 2, reverse sc] across, turn. Fasten off.

Row 2: Join buff with sc in first st, [ch 2, reverse sc in next ch sp] across with (ch 2, reverse sc) twice in each corner ch sp, turn. Fasten off.

Rows 3–8: Working in color sequence of sage, variegated, buff, burgundy, variegated and buff, rep row 2.

Row 9: Join navy with sc in end of row 1 on right-hand side, ch 1, sk next 2 rows, reverse sc in next row, ch 1, sk next 2 rows, reverse sc in next row, ch 1, sk last row, [reverse sc, ch 1] in each ch sp across with (reverse sc, ch 1) twice in each corner ch sp, ch 1, sk next row, [reverse sc in next row, ch 1, sk next 2 rows] twice, reverse sc in last row. Fasten off.

Overlapping right side of Neck Border over left side, sew ends of Border to Sides.

Sew 2 buttons 2½ inches apart to inside of Neck Border on right Side 1½ inches from outer edge and first button ½ inch from top edge.

Sew rem button to outside of Neck Border over corner sps of rnds 2 and 3 on left Side.

OUTER BORDER

Rnd 1: Working in ends of rows and in starting ch on opposite side of row 1 on Sides, join variegated with sc at back seam, ch 2, evenly sp sts so piece lays flat, working from left to right, [reverse sc, ch 2] around with (reverse sc, ch 2) twice in each corner, join with sl st in first sc, turn. Fasten off.

Rnd 2: Join buff with sc in first ch-1 sp, ch 2, [reverse sc in next ch sp, ch 2] around with (reverse sc, ch 2) twice in each corner ch sp, join, turn. Fasten off.

Rows 3–8: Working in color sequence of sage, variegated, buff, burgundy, variegated, buff and navy, rep rnd 2. ❑❑

Amazingly Simple

Design by Kathleen Sams for Coats & Clark

SKILL LEVEL
■■□□ EASY

FINISHED SIZE
One size fits most

MATERIALS
- ❑ Casual Cot'n Blend™ 29 percent cotton/61 percent acrylic/10 percent polyester bulky weight yarn from Red Heart☐ (140 yds/4oz per skein): **5 BULKY**
    - 3 skeins majestic #3339 (MC)
- ❑ Moda Dea™ Tiara 100 percent polyester super bulky weight yarn from Coats & Clark (46 yds/1.76 oz per ball): **6 SUPER BULKY**
    - 1 ball black out #4955 (CC)
- ❑ Size 15 (10mm) circular knitting needle or size needed to obtain gauge
- ❑ Size K/10½ (6.5mm) crochet hook

GAUGE
14 sts and 16 rows = 4 inches/10cm in pat st
To save time, take time to check gauge.

PATTERN NOTES
Circular needle is used to accommodate large number of sts. Do not join; work in rows.
Poncho is worked in 2 rectangular pieces, then sewn together.

FRONT/BACK
With MC, cast on 60 sts.
Row 1: Knit.
Row 2: *K1, k1-tbl; rep from * to last 2 sts, K2.
Rep Row 2 until piece measures 26 inches from beg.
Bind off.

ASSEMBLY
Lightly block both pieces to measure approx 16 x 26 inches
With RS facing, mark right side edge of front and back 9 inches below bound-off edge. This forms neck opening.
Referring to Fig.1, beg at lower edge and sew bound-off edge of back to side edge of front to marker, easing to fit.
Starting at lower edge, sew bound-off edge of front to side edge of back to marker, easing to fit.

EDGING
Rnd 1: With crochet hook and CC, attach yarn at seam, ch 1, sc around entire lower edge, working 3 sc in each corner and making sure to keep work flat. Join with sl st.
Rnds 2 and 3: Ch 1, sc in same st and in each st of previous rnd.
Join with sl st and fasten off.❑❑

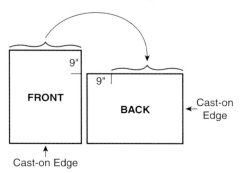

Fig. 1

Cozy & Cabled

Design by Melissa Leapman

SKILL LEVEL
■■■□ INTERMEDIATE

FINISHED SIZE
One size fits most

FINISHED MEASUREMENTS
Approx 52 inches wide x 30 inches long

MATERIALS
❏ Wool-Ease Thick & Quick [5 BULKY] 86 percent acrylic/ 10 percent wool/ 4 percent rayon bulky weight yarn from Lion Brand (6 oz/ 108 yds per skein):
  14 skeins wheat #402
❏ Size 13 (9mm) needles or size needed to obtain gauge
❏ Cable needle
❏ Stitch markers
❏ Stitch holders

GAUGE
10 sts and 14 rows = 4 inches/10cm in St st
To save time, take time to check gauge.

SPECIAL ABBREVATIONS
(CB) Cable Back: Slip 3 sts to cn and hold in back, k3, k3 from cn.
(CF) Cable Front: Slip 3 sts to cable needle and hold in front, k3, k3 from cn.

BACK
Cast on 130 sts.
Ribbing row: *K1, p1; rep from * across.
Rep Ribbing row until ribbing measures 2", ending with a WS row.

SET UP BODY PAT
Row 1 (RS): K37, pm, p1, k12, p1, pm, k28, pm, P1, K12, P1, pm, k37.
Row 2: [Purl to marker; k1, p12, k1] twice, purl to end of row.
Rows 3–6: Rep Rows 1 and 2.
Row 7: [Knit to marker; p1, CB, CF, p1] twice, knit to end of row.
Row 8: Rep Row 2.
[Rep Rows 1–8] 11 times more.
Rep Rows 1–4.
Next row (RS): Bind off 55 sts, work in pat to end of row.
Row 2: Bind off 55 sts, purl to end of row.
Place rem 20 sts on holder.

FRONT
Work as for back until 88 rows (11 pat reps) have been completed.
Rep Rows 1–2.
Shape neckline
Row 1: Knit to first marker; p1, k12, p1, k10, sl next 4 sts to holder, sl following 4 sts to 2nd holder; join 2nd ball of yarn, k10, p1, k12, p1, knit to end of row–61 sts on each side.
Continuing in established pat and working on both sides of neck with separate balls of yarn, bind off [2 sts at each neck edge] twice–57 sts each side.
Next row (RS): Knit to first marker, p1, k12, p1, k3, k2 tog, k1; on next side, k1, ssk, k3, p1, k12, p1; knit to end of row.
Row 2: Purl to first marker, k1, p12, k1, p2, p2 tog, p1; on next side, p1, p2 tog-tbl, p2, k1, p12, k1, purl to end of row —55 sts on each side.
Work even in established pat for 4 more rows.
Bind off all sts.

Sew shoulder seams.

SIDE BANDS
With RS facing, pick up and k 166 sts along arm edge of poncho.
Work even in k1, p1 ribbing for 2", ending with a WS row.
Bind off in ribbing.
Rep for other side.

HOOD
With RS facing, beg at center front, k4 from right neck holder, pm, pick up and knit 13 sts along right neck edge, knit across 20 sts of back neck holder, pick up and knit 13 sts along left neck edge, pm, k4 from left neck holder–54 sts.
Row 1 (WS): Sl 1, k1, p1, k1, purl to marker, [k1, p1] twice.
Row 2: Sl 1, p1, k1, p1, knit to marker, [p1, k1] twice.
Rep Rows 1 and 2 until hood measures 8½ inches from neck edge, ending with a WS row.

Top shaping
Row 1 (RS): Sl 1, p1, k1, p1, k21, ssk, pm, k2 tog; k21, [p1, k1] twice.
Row 2: Sl 1, k1, p1, k1, purl to last 4 sts, [p1, k1] twice.
Row 3: Sl 1, p1, k1, p1, knit to 2 sts before center marker, ssk, k2tog; knit to last 4 sts [p1, k1] twice.
[Rep Rows 2 and 3] 4 times more—42 sts.
Bind off in pattern.
Fold hood in half and sew top seam.❏❏

Embroidery Print

Design by Mary Layfield

SKILL LEVEL
INTERMEDIATE

FINISHED SIZE
One size fits most

MATERIALS
- Caron Simply Soft medium (worsted) weight yarn:
  20 oz/1,000 yds/567g #9811 embroidery print
  18 oz/900 yds/510g #9727 black
- Size G/6/4mm crochet hook or size needed to obtain gauge
- Tapestry needle

GAUGE
4 dc = 1 inch, 2 dc rows = 1 inch
Take time to check gauge.

PATTERN NOTES
All rows are worked from same side.
Do not turn rows.
Leave 5 inches of yarn at each end.

INSTRUCTIONS
SIDE
Make 2.
Row 1: Leaving 5-in end *(see Pattern Notes),* with black, ch 149, leaving 5-in end. Fasten off *(see Pattern Notes).* *(149 chs made)*
Row 2: Join black with sc in first ch, sc in next ch, ch 1, [sk next ch, sc in each of next 3 chs, ch 1] 36 times, sk next ch, sc in each of last 2 chs. Fasten off. *(112 sc)*
Row 3: Join black with sl st in first st, ch 3 *(counts as first dc),* dc in each st and ch across. Fasten off.
Row 4: Join black with sc in first st, sc in each st across. Fasten off.
Row 5: Join black with sl st in first st, ch 3 *(counts as first dc),* dc in next st, [ch 1, sk next st, dc in each of next 3 sts] 36 times, ch 1, sk next st, dc

in each of last 2 sts. Fasten off.
Row 6: Join print with sc in first st, sc in next st, [tr in sk st of row before last, sc in each of next 3 sts] 36 times, tr in next sk st on row before last, sc in each of last 2 sts. Fasten off. *(149 sts)*
Row 7: Join black with sl st in first st, ch 3, dc in each of next 3 sts, [ch 1, sk next st, dc in each of next 3 sts] 36 times, dc in last st. Fasten off.
Row 8: Join print with sc in first st, sc in each of next 3 sts, tr in sk st on row before last, [sc in each of next 3 sts, tr in sk st on row before last] 36 times, sc in each of last 4 sts. Fasten off.
Rows 9 & 10: Rep rows 5 and 6.
Row 11: Rep row 7.
Row 12: Join black with sl st in first st, ch 3, dc in next st, ch 1, sk next st, [dc in next st, dc in next ch sp, dc in next st, ch 1, sk next st] across to last 2 sts, dc in each of last 2 sts. Fasten off.
Row 13: Join black with sl st in first st, ch 3, dc in next st, dc in next ch sp, dc in next st, [ch 1, sk next st, dc in next st, dc in next ch sp, dc in next st] across with dc in last st. Fasten off.
Row 14: With black, rep row 12.
Row 15: With print, rep row 6.
Row 16: With black rep row 7.
Row 17: With print, rep row 8.
Rows 18 & 19: With print, rep rows 11 and 12.
Row 20: With black, rep row 6.
Row 21: With print, rep row 4.
Row 22: With black, rep row 3.
Row 23: With print, rep row 3.
Row 24: With black, rep row 3.
Row 25: With print, rep row 4.
Row 26: With black, rep row 5.
Row 27: With print, rep row 6.
Row 28: With print, rep row 7.
Row 29: With print, rep row 12.
Row 30: With black, rep row 13.

Row 31: With black, rep row 12.
Row 32: With black, rep row 13.
Row 33: With black, rep row 12.
Row 34: With print, rep row 6.
Row 35: With black, rep row 7.
Row 36: With print, rep row 8.
Row 37: With black, rep row 5.
Row 38: With print, rep row 6.
Row 39: For **shoulder shaping,** join black with sl st in first st, ch 3, dc in each of next 23 sts, [sk next st, dc in each of next 2 sts] 7 times, dc in each st across. Fasten off. *(142 dc)*
Row 40: Join black with sl st in first st, ch 3, dc in each of next 21 sts, [sk next st, dc in each of next 2 sts] 7 times, dc in each st across. Fasten off. *(135 dc)*
Row 41: Join black with sl st in first st, ch 3, dc in each of next 20 sts, [sk next st, dc in each of next 2 sts] 6 times, dc in each st across. Fasten off. *(129 dc)*
Row 42: Join black with sl st in first st, ch 3, dc in next st, [ch 1, sk next st, dc in each of next 3 sts] 31 times, ch 1, sk next st, dc in each of last 2 sts. Fasten off.
Row 43: Join print with sc in first st, sc in next st, [tr in sk st of row before last, sc in each of next 3 sts] 31 times, tr in next sk st of row before last, sc in each of last 2 sts. Fasten off. *(129 sts)*
Row 44: Working on opposite side of starting ch of row 1, with black, rep row 4.
Row 45: With black, rep row 5.
Row 46: With print, rep row 6.
Sew pieces tog according to illustration on page 29, sewing behind last print row.

FRINGE
Cut 5 strands print each 10 inches long. Holding all strands tog, fold in half, pull fold through, pull ends through fold. Pull to tighten.
Fringe in each tr around bottom edge. Trim ends.❑❑

Long & Cozy

Design by Chris Adams

SKILL LEVEL

■■■□ INTERMEDIATE

FINISHED SIZE

41½ x 37 inches long from shoulder to bottom, not including Fringe

MATERIALS

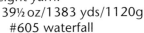

❑ Bernat Illusions by Spinrite bulky (chunky) weight yarn:
   39½ oz/1383 yds/1120g #605 waterfall
❑ Size N/13/9mm crochet hook or size needed to obtain gauge

GAUGE

2 hdc = 1 inch, rows 1–12 = 7 inches
Take time to check gauge.

SPECIAL STITCHES

Front post half double crochet (fphdc): yo, insert hook from front to back around post (see Stitch Guide) of next st, yo, pull lp through, yo, pull through all lps on hook.

Back post half double crochet (bphdc): Yo, insert hook from back to front around post of next st, yo, pull lp through, yo, pull through all lps on hook.

INSTRUCTIONS

PONCHO

Row 1: Ch 84, hdc in 3rd ch from hook, hdc in each ch across, turn. (83 hdc)

Row 2: Ch 2 (counts as first hdc throughout), **fphdc** (see Special Stitches) around each st across, turn.

Row 3: Ch 2, hdc in each st across, turn.

Row 4: Ch 2, **bphdc** (see Special Stitches) around each st across, turn.

Row 5: Ch 2, hdc in each st across, turn.

Rows 6–13: Rep rows 2–5 consecutively.

Row 14: Ch 2, bphdc around each of next 4 sts, [fphdc around next st, bphdc around each of next 5 sts] across, turn.

Row 15: Ch 2, hdc in each st across, turn.

Rows 16–25: Rep rows 14 and 15 alternately.

Rows 26–37: Rep rows 2–5 consecutively.

Rows 38–53: Ch 2, hdc in each st across, turn.

Row 54: Ch 2, hdc in each of next 25 sts, for **neck opening**, ch 32, sk next 32 sts, hdc in each of last 25 sts, turn. (51 hdc, 32 chs)

Row 55: Ch 2, hdc in each st and in each ch across, turn. (83 hdc)

Rows 56–73: Ch 2, hdc in each st across, turn.

Row 74: Ch 2, bphdc around each st across, turn.

Row 75: Ch 2, hdc in each st across, turn.

Row 76: Ch 2, fphdc around each st across, turn.

Row 77: Ch 2, hdc in each st across, turn.

Rows 78–85: Rep rows 74–77 consecutively.

Rows 86–97: Rep rows 14 and 15 alternately.

Rows 98–109: Rep rows 74–77 consecutively.

Row 110: Ch 2, hdc in each st across, turn. **Do not fasten off.**

OUTER EDGING

Rnd 1: Ch 1, 2 sc in first st, sc in each of next 81 sts, 3 sc in last st; *working in ends of rows, sc in each of first 9 rows, 2 sc in next row, [sc in each of next 12 rows, 2 sc in next row] 7 times, sc in each of last 9 rows*; working in starting ch on opposite side of row 1, 3 sc in first ch, sc in each of next 81 chs, 3 sc in last ch, rep between *, sc in same st as first st, join with sl st in beg sc.

Rnd 2: Ch 1, 2 sc in first st, sc in each st around with 3 sc in each center corner st, sc in same st as first st, join with sl st in beg sc. Fasten off.

NECK EDGING

Rnd 1: Working around neck opening, join with sc in 17th sk st on row 53, sc in each of next 15 sts, sc in end of next row, sc in each of next 32 chs, sc in end of next row, sc in each of last 16 sts, join with sl st in beg sc, **turn.**

Row 2: Working in rows, ch 3, sk next st, hdc in next st, [ch 1, sk next st, hdc in next st] across, turn.

Row 3: Ch 1, sc in each st and each ch across, turn. Fasten off.

For **tie,** cut 3 strands yarn each 45 inches in length. Holding all 3 strands together, starting 14 inches from each end, tie 4 knots evenly sp across. Weave through ch sps of row 2. Tie ends into a bow.

FRINGE

For each fringe, cut 1 strand yarn 18 inches in length. Fold in half, insert hook in st, pull fold through st, pull loose ends through fold, tighten. Trim ends.

Fringe in each st across each bottom edge of Poncho.❏❏

Textured Cable

Design by Agnes Russell

FINISHED SIZES

Instructions for Ladies small, changes for medium and large are in [ ]

MATERIALS

❏ Red Heart Super Saver medium (worsted) weight yarn:
  14 [16, 18] oz/700 [800, 100] yds/397 [425, 510]g each #4996 ragg and #400 gray heather
❏ Size N/15/10mm crochet hook or size needed to obtain gauge
❏ Tapestry needle
❏ 8 [9, 10] 15mm decorative shank buttons

GAUGE

5 sc = 1 inch, 4 sc rnds = 1 inch
Take time to check gauge.

PATTERN NOTES

Work with 1 strand of each color held together throughout pattern.

Poncho is crocheted from neckline down. Neckline trim is added later.

If a solid-color poncho is desired, purchase 28 [32, 36] oz of the same color.

Poncho can be made larger in multiples of 5 sts. Each multiple adds 1 sc and 4 sts for cable.

Purchase sufficient yarn for larger poncho.

SPECIAL STITCHES

Front post double crochet (fpdc): Yo, insert hook around post *(see Stitch Guide)* of st, yo, pull lp through, complete as dc.

Back post double crochet (bpdc): Yo, insert hook around post *(see Stitch Guide)* of st, yo, pull lp through, complete as dc.

Front post double crochet cable twist (fpdc cable twist): Sk next 2 sts, **fpdc** *(see Special Stitches)* around each of next 2 sts, fpdc around first sk st, fpdc around 2nd sk st.

Front post single crochet (fpsc): Insert hook front to back to front again around l post of indicated st, yo, complete sc.

Front post half double crochet (fphdc): Yo, insert hook front to back to front again around post of indicated st, yo, pull up lp, yo, pull through all lps on hook.

Back post half double crochet (bphdc): Yo, insert hook back to front to back again around post of indicated st, yo, pull up lp, yo, pull through all lps on hook.

Increase (inc): 2 sc in indicated st.

INSTRUCTIONS

PONCHO

Rnd 1 (RS): With 1 strand each color, ch 40 [45, 50], sl st in first ch to form ring, ch 1, sc in each ch around, join with sl st in beg sc, **turn.** *(40 [45, 50] sc)*

Rnd 2 (WS): Ch 1, sc in each st around, join with sl st in beg sc, turn.

Rnd 3: Ch 1, sc in first st, *fpdc *(see Special Stitches)* around each of next 4 sc of rnd 1, sk 4 sc directly behind fpdc sts**, sc in next sc of rnd 2, rep from * around, ending last rep at **, join with sl st in beg sc, turn. *(8 [9, 10] s, 8 [9, 10] groups of 4 fpdc sts)*

Rnd 4: Ch 1, sc in first sc, *bpdc *(see Special Stitches)* around each of next 4 fpdc sts**, 2 sc in next sc, rep from * around, ending last rep at **, sc in same sc as beg sc, join with sl st in beg sc, turn. *(50 [55, 60] sts)*

Rnd 5: Ch 1, sc in first sc, *fpdc cable twist *(see Special Stitches)* over next 4 bpdc sts, 2 sc in next sc**, sc in next sc, rep from * around, ending last rep at **, join with sl st in beg sc, turn. *(60 [65, 70] sts)*

Rnd 6: Ch 1, [sc in each sc, bpdc around each fpdc] around, join with sl st in beg sc, turn.

Rnd 7: Ch 1, **inc** 1 sc (see Special Stitches) across each sc section, fpdc around each bpdc st, join, turn. (70, [75, 80] sts)

Rnd 8: Rep rnd 6.

Rnd 9: Ch 1, inc 1 sc across each sc section, fpdc cable twist over each section of 4 bpdc sts, join with sl st in beg sc, turn. (80 [85, 90] sts)

Rnd 10: Rep rnd 6.

Rnd 11: Ch 1, sc in each sc and fpdc around each bpdc st around, join with sl st in beg sc, turn.

Rnd 12: Rep rnd 6.

Rnd 13: Rep rnd 9. (90 [96, 100] sts)

Rnd 14: Rep rnd 6.

Rnd 15: Rep rnd 7. (100 [105, 110] sts)

Rnd 16: Rep rnd 6.

Rnd 17: Ch 1, [sc in each sc, fpdc cable twist around 4 bpdc sts] around, join with sl st in beg sc, turn.

Rnd 18: Rep rnd 6.

Rnd 19: Rep rnd 11.

Rnd 20: Rep rnd 6.

Rnd 21: Rep rnd 9. (110 [115, 120] sts)

Rnd 22: Rep rnd 6.

Rnd 23: Rep rnd 11.

Rnd 24: Rep rnd 6.

Rnd 25: Rep rnd 17.

Rnd 26: Rep rnd 6.

Rnd 27: Rep rnd 11.

Rnd 28: Rep rnd 6.

Rnd 29: Rep rnd 9. (120 [125, 130] sts)

Rnds 30–41: Rep rnds 22–25.

Rnd 42: Rep rnd 6.

Rnd 43: Ch 1, sc in each sc and **fpsc** (see Special Stitches) around each bpdc st around, join with sl st in beg sc, **do not turn.**

Rnd 44: Ch 1, working from left to right, **reverse sc** (see illustration) in each st around, join with sl st in beg sc. Fasten off.

Reverse Single Crochet

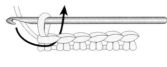
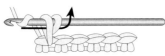

NECKLINE TRIM

Rnd 1 (RS): Working in starting ch on opposite side of row 1, join 1 strand each color with sl st in first ch, ch 1, sc in each ch around, join with sl st in beg sc, **do not turn.** (40 [45, 50] sc)

Rnd 2: Ch 1 loosely, [fphdc around next sc, bphdc around next sc] around, join with sl st in top of beg fphdc.

Rnds 3–5: Ch 1 loosely, [fphdc around each fphdc, bphdc around each bphdc] around, join with sl st in top of beg fphdc,

Rnd 6: Ch 1, reverse sc in each st around, join with sl st in beg sc. Fasten off.

FINISHING

Sew 1 button over rnd 1 of Poncho, centered over each cable. Using natural sps for buttonholes, pass each button through rnd 5 of neckline trim. Depending upon the weather, wear buttoned or unbuttoned.❑❑

Cozy Warmth

Design by Sue Childress

FINISHED SIZE
One size fits most

FINISHED MEASUREMENTS
Approx 23 inches long

MATERIALS
- ❑ Kayek 75 percent wool/18 percent acrylic/ 7 percent mohair super bulky weight yarn from Grignasco (38 yds/50g per ball): 12 balls #170 (MC)
- ❑ Baby 100 percent Merino wool super bulky yarn from Tahki Stacy Charles Inc. (60 yds /100g per ball): 2 balls cream #1 (CC)
- ❑ Size 15 (10mm) 29- and 36-inch circular needles or size needed to obtain gauge
- ❑ Stitch markers

GAUGE
10 sts and 12 rnds = 4 inches/10cm in St st
To save time, take time to check gauge.

SPECIAL ABBREVIATIONS
Double inc: Knit to 1 st before marked st, k1 in top of st in row below st on needle, k3 (marked st is in center), k1 in top of st in row below st just knit. (2 sts inc)

PATTERN NOTES
Circular needle is used to accommodate large number of sts. Do not join; work in rows. Change to longer needle when necessary.
Use safety pin type markers; move marker up as you work to keep inc line consistent.
Inc rnds will beg 1 st before first marked st.

PONCHO
With shorter needle and MC, cast on 52 sts. Join without twisting, pm between first and last st.

Rnds 1–3: *K2, p2; rep from * around.
Rnd 4: Knit.
Rnd 5: [K1, pm in this st, k12] 3 times, k1, pm in this st, k11.
Rnd 6: *Work double inc, knit to 1 st before next marker; rep from * around – 8 sts increased.
Rnd 7: Knit, ending 1 st before first marked st.
Rep Rnds 6 and 7 until poncho measures approx 10 inches.
Next 2 rnds: Knit.
Next rnd: *Work double inc, knit to 1 st before next marker; rep from * around.

Rep last 3 rnds until poncho measures approx 21 inches.
Cut MC, change to CC.

BORDER
Knit 1 rnd, purl 3 rnds.
Bind off purlwise.❑❑

Plum Stripes

Design by Agnes Russell

SKILL LEVEL

■■■□ INTERMEDIATE

FINISHED SIZE
Girl's sizes 8–10

MATERIALS
❑ Textured chunky yarn (3½ oz/175 yds/99g per ball):
2 balls each solid color (MC) and variegated color (CC)

❑ Size P/15/10mm double-ended crochet hook or size needed to obtain gauge
❑ Size P/15/10mm crochet hook
❑ Tapestry needle
❑ 5-inch square of cardboard

GAUGE
4 sts = 2 inches
Take time to check gauge.

PATTERN NOTE
Poncho is crocheted in two simple strips.

To **pull up lp**, insert hook in vertical bar, yo, pull lp through leaving lps on hook.

When **picking up lps,** leave all lps on hook unless otherwise stated.

To **turn,** rotate hook 180 degrees and slide all lps to opposite end. Do not turn unless otherwise stated.

To **work lps off hook when adding a new color,** with new color, place sl knot on hook, pull sp knot through first lp on hook, [yo, pull through 2 lps on hook] across.

To **work lps off with color already in use,** pick up color from row below, yo, pull through 1 lp on hook, [yo, pull through 2 lps on hook] across.

You will always have 1 lp left on your hook at the end after working lps off, this will be the first st of the next row.

INSTRUCTIONS

PONCHO
FIRST HALF

Row 1: With double-ended hook and MC, ch 25, insert hook in 2nd ch from hook, pull up lp (see Pattern Notes), pull up lp in each ch across, turn, slide all lps to opposite end of hook. (25 lps on hook)

Row 2: With CC, work lps off hook, **do not turn.**

Row 3: Sk first vertical bar, pull up lp in each vertical bar across, turn.

Row 4: With MC, work lps off hook across, **do not turn.**

Row 5: Sk first vertical bar, pull up lp in each vertical bar across, turn.

Row 6: With CC, work lps off hook across, **do not turn.**

Row 7: Sk first vertical bar, pull up lp in each vertical bar across, turn.

Rows 8–102: Rep rows 4–7.

Row 103: Continuing with CC, sk first vertical bar, sl st in each vertical bar across. Fasten off.

SECOND HALF

Row 1: With predominately MC facing and using diagram as a guide, beginning with row 1 of First Half, make a slip knot with MC and pick up 25 lps along edge as indicated.

Rows 2–103: Rep rows 2–103 of First Half.

With predominantly MC facing and using diagram as a guide, sew seam joining at A and B.

BOTTOM TRIM

With predominately CC facing, with size P crochet hook, join MC with sl st at back seam, ch 1, evenly sp sc around, working 3 sc in each corner, join with sl st in beg sc. Fasten off.

NECKLINE TRIM

Note: *This edging is designed to create a rolled edging around the neckline.*

Rnd 1: With predominately CC side facing and size P crochet hook, join MC with sl st, ch 1, work 52 sc evenly sp around neckline opening, join with sl st in beg sc. *(52 sc)*

Rnds 2–4: Working in **front lps** *(see Stitch Guide)* only, sl st in each st

around, **do not join.** At the end of last rnd, fasten off.

Rnd 5: Turn Poncho inside out, with size P crochet hook, join MC in unworked lps of rnd 1 of neckline trim, working with a slightly tighter tension to give neck stability, sl st in each st around. Fasten off.

TIE

With CC and size P crochet hook, leaving a 6-in length at beg, ch 50. Leaving a 6-in length, fasten off.

Fold tie in half, insert hook at center front of Poncho in rnd 2 of neckline trim, pull fold through, pull ends through fold, pull to secure.

POMPOM
Make 2.

From cardboard, cut 2 circles 2¼-inches in diameter, cut 1-inch hole in center of each circle. Holding the cardboard circles tog, wrap CC yarn around the cardboard circles until center hole is filled. Insert scissors between

layers of cardboard circles, gently cut around outer edge between circles. Cut a separate length of CC yarn, place between cardboard circles, pull ends tightly and knot to secure. Remove cardboard circles and attach pompom to end of Tie. Make 2nd pompom and attach to rem end of Tie.❑❑

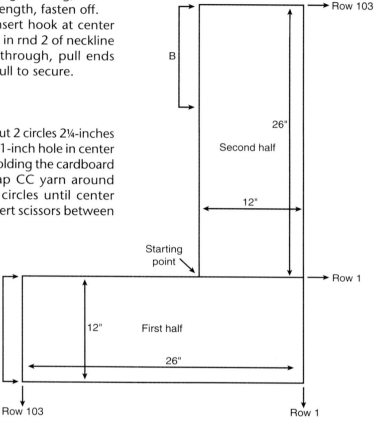

Bobbles & Shells

Design by Sharon Hatfield

SKILL LEVEL
■■■□ INTERMEDIATE

FINISHED SIZES
Instructions given for 2–3 year old child, changes for 4–5 year old are in [ ]. Rows rep for larger size child to add length.

MATERIALS
❏ Red Heart Kids or medium (worsted) weight yarn:
  7 oz/350 yds/198g #2230 yellow
  3 oz/150 yds/85g #2945 bikini
❏ Sizes H/8/5mm and I/9/5.5mm crochet hooks or sizes needed to obtain gauge
❏ Tapestry needle
❏ 4–inch square piece of cardboard

GAUGE
Size H hook: 4 sc = 1 inch, 7 sc back lp rows = 2 inches
Size I hook: 3 dc = 1 inch, 4 dc rows = 2½ inches
Take time to check gauge.

SPECIAL STITCHES
Beginning popcorn (beg pc): Ch 3 (counts as first dc), 2 dc in same st, drop lp from hook, insert hook in top of ch-3, pull dropped lp through.
Popcorn (pc): 3 dc in next st, drop lp from hook, insert hook in first dc of 3-dc group, pull dropped lp through.

INSTRUCTIONS
PONCHO
NECKBAND
Row 1: With size H hook and bikini, ch 5, sc in 2nd ch from hook and in each ch across, turn. (4 sc)
Rows 2–48: Working the following rows in **back lps** (see Stitch Guide), ch 1, sc in each st across, turn. At end of last row, leaving 8–inch end for sewing, fasten off.
Sew first and last rows tog through back lps.

BODY
Rnd 1: With size I hook and yellow, join with sc in end of first row on Neckband, sc in end of each row around, join with sl st in beg sc. (48 sc)
Rnd 2: Ch 3 (counts as first dc throughout), dc in same st, 2 dc in each st around, join with sl st in 3rd ch of beg ch-3. (96 dc)
Rnd 3: Ch 3, dc in each st around, join with sl st in 3rd ch of beg ch-3. Fasten off.
Rnd 4: Join bikini with sl st in first st, **beg pc** (see Special Stitches), sc in each of next 3 sts, *pc (see Special Stitches) in next st, sc in each of next 3 sts, rep from * around, join with sl st in 3rd ch of beg pc. Fasten off.
Rnd 5: Join yellow with sl st in first st, ch 3, dc in each st around, join with sl st in 3rd ch of beg ch-3.
Rnds 6–7: Ch 3, dc in each st around, join with sl st in 3rd ch of beg ch-3. At end of last rnd, fasten off.
Rnds 8–15: Rep rnds 4–7 consecutively.
Rnd 16: Join bikini with sl st in first st, (ch 3, 4 dc) in same st, sk next st, sc in next st, sk next st, [5 dc in next st, sk next st, sc in next st, sk next st] around, join with sl st in 3rd ch of beg ch-3. Fasten off.

HAT
HATBAND
Row 1: With size H hook and bikini, ch 7, sc in 2nd ch from hook and in each ch across, turn. (6 sc)
Rows 2–48 [2–52]: Working the following rows in back lps only, ch 1, sc in each st across, turn. At end of last row, leaving 8–inch end for sewing, fasten off.
Sew first and last rows tog through back lps.

CROWN
Rnd 1: With size I hook and yellow, join with sc in end of first row on Hatband, sc in end of each row around, join with sl st in beg sc. (48 [52] sc)

Rnd 2: Ch 3, dc in each st around, join with sl st in 3rd ch of beg ch-3. Fasten off.
Rnd 3: Join bikini with sl st in first st, beg pc, sc in each of next 3 sts, [pc in next st, sc in each of next 3 sts] around, join with sl st in 3rd ch of beg pc. Fasten off.
Rnd 4: Join yellow with sl st in first st, ch 3, dc in each st around, join with sl st in 3rd ch of beg ch-3. Fasten off.
Rnds 5–10: Repeat rnds 3 and 4 alternately. At end of last rnd, **do not fasten off.**
Rnd 11: Ch 3, dc in each st around, join with sl st in 3rd ch of beg ch-3.
Rnd 12: Working this rnd in back lps only, ch 3, dc in each st around, join with sl st in 3rd ch of beg ch-3.
Rnds 13–15 [13–14]: Ch 1, **sc dec** (see Stitch Guide) in first 2 sts, [sc dec in next 2 sts] around, join with

sl st in beg sc, ending with 6 [13] sc in last rnd.

[Rnd 15]: For size 4–5 year old only, ch 1, sk first st, [sc dec in next 2 sts] around, join with sl st in beg sc. *[6 sc]*

Rnd 16 [16]: For **all sizes,** ch 1, sc dec in first 2 sts, [sc dec in next 2 sts] around, join with sl st in beg sc. Fasten off.
Fold Hatband up.

POMPOM
Wrap bikini around cardboard 80 times, slide loops off cardboard, tie separate strand around middle of all loops. Cut loops. Trim ends. Sew to top of Hat.❑❑

CROCHET

Sweet Dreams

Design by Glenda Winkleman

SKILL LEVEL
■■■□ INTERMEDIATE

FINISHED SIZES
Instructions for 0–6 months, changes for 12 months and 18–24 months are in [ ]

MATERIALS
❑ Red Heart Baby Teri medium (worsted) weight yarn (3 oz/200 yds/85g per skein):
  2 skeins #9121 yellow
  1 skein each #9137 pink, #9181 blue, #9180 mint and #9145 lilac
❑ Size I/9/5.5mm afghan crochet hook or size needed to obtain gauge
❑ Sizes H/8/5mm crochet hook
❑ Tapestry needle

GAUGE
Afghan hook: 8 sts = 2 inches, 6 rows = 2 inches
Take time to check gauge.

PATTERN NOTES
For each size Poncho work a total of 36 squares.
Squares measure 2½ inches for size 6 months, 2¾ inches for size 12 months and 3 inches for size 18–24 months.

PATTERN STITCH
Afghan stitch (see illustrations):
[Insert hook under next vertical bar, yo, pull up lp] across to last bar leaving all lps on hook, for last st, insert hook under last bar and st directly behind it, yo, pull through bar and lp, to **work lps off hook** yo, pull through first lp

on hook, [yo, pull through 2 lps on hook] across leaving last lp on hook.

INSTRUCTIONS
PONCHO
SQUARE
Make 36.
Row 1: With size I afghan hook and pink, ch 9 [11, 13], insert hook in 2nd ch from hook, yo, pull up lp, [insert hook in next ch, yo, pull up lp] across leaving all lps on hook, work lps off hook, yo, pull through 1 lp on hook, [yo, pull through 2 lps on hook] across leaving last lp on hook, changing to yellow before last lp is pull through, last lp counts as first lp of next row. Fasten off pink.

Row 2: With yellow, first lp counts as first st, [with yarn in front of work on right-hand side of next vertical bar, insert hook in next vertical bar, yarn underneath and to the back of hook, yo, pull lp through, with yarn at back of work, insert hook in next vertical bar, yo, pull lp through] across, work lps off hook, yo, pull through first lp on hook, [yo, pull through 2 lps on hook] across changing to mint before last lp is pulled through leaving last lp on hook. **Do not fasten off** yellow, carry yellow behind work throughout pattern.

Row 3: With mint, first lp counts as regular afghan st, [with yarn to the back of work, insert hook in next vertical bar, pull lp through, With yarn in front of work on right-hand side of next vertical bar, insert hook in next vertical bar, place yarn underneath and to the back of hook, yo, pull lp through st[across to with last 2 sts, with yarn at back, work last 2 sts in afghan st, work lps off hook, yo, pull through first lp on hook, [yo, pull through 2 lps on hook] across leaving last lp on hook.
Row 4: With yellow, rep row 2.
Row 5: With blue rep row 3.
Row 6: With yellow, rep row 2,
Row [7, 7]: With lilac, rep row 3,
Row [, 8]: With yellow, rep row 2.
Row 7 [8, 9]: Sl st in each vertical st across. Fasten off.

ASSEMBLY

Using diagram as a guide, sew Squares tog.

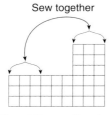

Sew together

**Sweet Dreams Poncho
Assembly Chart**

BOTTOM BORDER

Rnd 1 (RS): With size H hook, join lilac with sl st in center bottom point of front of Poncho, ch 1, 3 sc in point st, sc in each st around bottom edge of Poncho with 3 sc in center back point, join with sl st in beg sc. Fasten off.

Rnd 2: Join yellow with sl st in first sc of previous rnd, ch 1, sc in same sc, ch 1, sk next sc, [sc in next sc, ch 1, sk next sc] around, join with sl st in beg sc. Fasten off.

Rnd 3: Join pink with sl st in first sc of previous rnd, ch 1, sc in same sc, *sc in next ch-1 sp, ch 3, sl st in top of last sc made**, sc in next sc, rep from * around, ending last rep at **, join with sl st in beg sc. Fasten off.

NECKLINE TRIM

Rnd 1 (RS): With size H hook, join lilac with sl st in front center st of neck opening, ch 1, evenly sp sc around neckline, join with sl st in beg sc. Fasten off.

Rnd 2: Join yellow with sl st in first sc of previous rnd, ch 1, sc in same sc, ch 1, sk next sc, [sc in next sc, ch 1, sk next sc] around, join with sl st in beg sc. Fasten off.

TIE

With size H hook and pink, ch 100, sc in 2nd ch from hook and in each ch across. Fasten off.

Starting and ending at front center neckline opening, weave tie through ch-1 sps of rnd 2, adjust tie ends evenly.❑❑

CROCHET

Vanilla Cream

Design by Mary Layfield

SKILL LEVEL
■■■□ INTERMEDIATE

FINISHED SIZE
One size fits most

MATERIALS
- ❑ Red Heart LusterSheen fine (sport) weight yarn: 12¼ oz/1,050 yds/350g #7 vanilla
- ❑ Size F/5/3.75mm crochet hook or size needed to obtain gauge
- ❑ Sewing needle
- ❑ Thread
- ❑ 6 pearl ⅝-inch buttons

2 FINE

GAUGE
5 dc = 1 inch, 4 dc rows = 1½ inches
Take time to check gauge.

INSTRUCTIONS

Row 1: Beg at neck, ch 97, sc in second ch from hook and in each ch across, turn. *(96 sc made)*

Row 2: Ch 1, sc in each of first 4 sts, 2 sc in next st, [sc in each of next 2 sts, 2 sc in next st] twice, **for shoulder,** sc in each of next 15 sts, 2 sc in each of next 2 sts, sc in each of next 40 sts, 2 sc in each of next 2 sts, **for shoulder,** sc in each of next 15 sts, 2 sc in next st, [sc in each of next 2 sts, 2 sc in next st] twice, sc in each of last 4 sts, turn. *(106 sc)*

Row 3: Ch 3 *(counts as first dc),* dc in each of next 4 sts, [sk next 3 sts, 5 dc in next st, ch 2, sk next 2 sts, dc in each of next 3 sts] 11 times, dc in each of last 2 sts, turn. *(95 dc, 11 ch sps)*

Row 4: Ch 3, dc in each of next 4 sts, [sk next ch sp, 5 dc in next st, ch 2, sk next 4 sts, dc in each of next 3 sts] across with dc in each of last 2 sts, turn.

Row 5: Ch 3, dc in each of next 4 sts, sk next ch sp, 5 dc in next st, ch 2, sk next 4 sts, [dc in next st, 2 dc in next st, dc in next st, sk next ch sp, 5 dc in next st, ch 2, sk next 4 sts] across with dc in each of last 5 sts, turn. *(105 dc, 11 ch sps)*

Row 6: Ch 3, dc in each of next 4 sts, sk next ch sp, 5 dc in next st, ch 2, sk next 4 sts, [dc in each of next 2 sts, ch 2, dc in each of next 2 sts, sk next st, 5 dc in next st, ch 2, sk next 4 sts] across with dc in each of last 5 sts, turn. *(105 dc, 21 ch sps)*

Row 7: Ch 3, dc next st, 2 dc in next st, dc in each of next 2 sts, sk next ch sp, 5 dc in next st, ch 2, sk next 4 sts, [dc in each of next 2 sts, 3 dc in next ch sp, dc in each of next 2 sts, sk next ch sp, 5 dc in next st, ch 2, sk next 4 sts] across to last 5 sts, dc in each of next 2 sts, 2 dc in next st, dc in each of last 2 sts, turn. *(137 dc)*

Row 8: Ch 3, dc in each of next 5 sts, sk next ch sp, 5 dc in next st, ch 2, sk next 4 sts, [dc in each of next 7 sts, sk next ch sp, 5 dc in next st, ch 2, sk next 4 sts] across with dc in each of last 6 sts, turn.

Row 9: Ch 3, dc in each of next 5 sts, sk next ch sp, 5 dc in next st, ch 2, sk next 4 sts, *[dc in next st, sk next st, dc in next st, dc in last sk st] twice, dc in next st, sk next ch sp, 5 dc in next st, ch 2, sk next 4 sts, rep from * across with dc in each of last 6 sts, turn.

Row 10: Ch 3, dc in each of next 5 sts, sk next ch sp, 5 dc in next st, ch 2, sk next 4 sts, [dc in next st, sk next st, dc in next st, dc in last sk st, 2 dc in next st, sk next st, dc in next st, dc in st just sk, dc in next st, sk next ch sp, 5 dc in next st, ch 2, sk next 4 sts] across with dc in each of last 6 sts, turn. *(147 dc)*

Row 11: Ch 3, dc in each of next 5 sts, sk next ch sp, 5 dc in next st, ch 2, sk next 4 sts, *dc in next st, ch 1, [sk next st, dc in next st, dc in last sk st, ch 1] 3 times, dc in next st, sk next ch sp, 5 dc in next st, ch 2, sk next 4 sts, rep from * across with dc in each of last 6 sts, turn.

Row 12: Ch 3, dc in each of next 5 sts, sk next ch sp, 5 dc in next st, ch 2, sk next 4 sts, [dc in next st, dc in next ch sp, dc in next st, ch 2, sk next st, ch sp and next st, dc in next st, dc in last sk st, ch 2, sk next ch sp and st, dc in next st, dc in next ch sp, dc in next st, sk next ch sp, 5 dc in next st, ch 2, sk next 4 sts] across with dc in each of last 6 sts, turn.

Row 13: Ch 3, dc in each of next 5 sts, sk next ch sp, 5 dc in next st, ch 2, sk next 4 sts, [dc in each of next 3 sts, ch 2, sk next st, dc in next st, dc in last sk st, ch 2, dc in each of next 3 sts, sk next ch sp, 5 dc in next st, ch 2, sk next 4 sts] across with dc in each of last 6 sts, turn.

Row 14: Ch 3, dc in each of next 5 sts, sk next ch sp, 5 dc in next st, ch 2, sk next 4 sts, [dc in each of next 3 sts, ch 3, sk next st, dc in next st, dc in last sk st, ch 3, dc in each of next 3 sts, sk next ch sp, 5 dc in next st, ch 2, sk next 4 sts] across with dc in each of last 6 sts, turn.

Row 15: Ch 3, dc in each of next 5 sts, sk next ch sp, 5 dc in next st, ch 2, sk next 4 sts, [dc in each of next 3 sts, ch 3, sk next st, dc in next st, dc in last sk st, ch 3, dc in each of next 3 sts, sk next ch sp, 5 dc in next st, ch 2, sk next 4 sts] across with dc in each of last 6 sts, turn.

Row 16: Ch 3, dc in each of next 5 sts, sk next ch sp, 5 dc in next st, ch 2, sk next 4 sts, [dc in each of next 3 sts, ch 4, sk next st, dc in next st, dc in last sk st, ch 4, dc in each of next 3 sts, sk next ch sp, 5 dc in next st, ch 2, sk next 4 sts] across with dc in each of last 6 sts, turn.

Row 17: Ch 3, dc in each of next 5 sts, sk next ch sp, 5 dc in next st, ch 2, sk next 4 sts, [dc in each of next 3 sts, ch 4, sk next st, dc in next st, dc in last sk st, ch 4, dc in each of next 3 sts, sk next ch sp, 5 dc in next st, ch 2, sk next 4 sts] across with dc in each of last 6 sts, turn.

Row 18: Ch 3, dc in each of next 5 sts, sk next ch sp, 5 dc in next st, ch 2, sk next 4 sts, [dc in next st, 2 dc in next st, dc in next st, ch 4, sk next st, dc in next st, dc in last sk st, ch 4, dc in next st, 2 dc in next st, dc in next st, sk next ch sp, 5 dc in next st, ch 2, sk next 4 sts] across with dc in each of last 6 sts, turn. *(167 dc)*

Row 19: Ch 3, dc in each of next 5 sts, sk next ch sp, 5 dc in next st, ch 2, sk next 4 sts, [dc in each of next 4 sts, ch 5, sk next st, dc in next st, dc in last sk st, ch 5, dc in each of next 4 sts, sk next ch sp, 5 dc in next st, ch 2, sk next 4 sts] across with dc in each of last 6 sts, turn.

Row 20: Ch 3, dc in each of next 5 sts, sk next ch sp, 5 dc in next st, ch 2, sk next 4 sts, [dc in each of next 4 sts, ch 5, sk next st, dc in next st, dc in last sk st, ch 5, dc in each of next 4 sts, sk next ch sp, 5 dc in next st, ch 2, sk next 4 sts] across with dc in each of last 6 sts, turn.

Row 21: Ch 3, dc in each of next 5 sts, sk next ch sp, 5 dc in next st, ch 2, sk next 4 sts, [dc in each of next 4 sts, ch 5, dc in next st, ch 1, dc in next st, ch 5, dc in each of next 4 sts, sk next ch sp, 5 dc in next st, ch 2, sk next

Row 22: Ch 3, dc in each of next 5 sts, sk next ch sp, 5 dc in next st, ch 2, sk next 4 sts, [dc in each of next 4 sts, ch 4, 5 dc in next ch-1 sp, ch 4, dc in each of next 4 sts, sk next ch sp, 5 dc in next st, ch 2, sk next 4 sts] across with dc in each of last 6 sts, turn. *(197 dc)*

Row 23: Ch 3, dc in each of next 5 sts, sk next ch sp, 5 dc in next st, ch 2, sk next 4 sts, [dc in each of next 4 sts, ch 3, 5 dc in next st, ch 3, sk next 3 sts, 5 dc in next st, ch 3, dc in each of next 4 sts, sk next ch sp, 5 dc in next st, ch 2, sk next 4 sts] across with dc in each of last 6 sts, turn. (247 dc)

Row 24: Ch 3, dc in each of next 5 sts, sk next ch sp, 5 dc in next st, ch 2, sk next 4 sts, [dc in each of next 4 sts, 5 dc in next st, ch 3, dc in next ch sp, ch 3, sk next 4 sts, 5 dc in next st, sk next ch sp, dc in each of next 4 sts, sk next ch sp, 5 dc in next st, ch 2, sk next 4 sts] across with dc in each of last 6 sts, turn. (257 dc)

Row 25: Ch 3, dc in each of next 5 sts, sk next ch sp, 5 dc in next st, ch 2, sk next 4 sts, [dc in each of next 4 sts, ch 3, sk next 2 sts, dc in next st, ch 3, sk next 2 sts and ch sp, 5 dc in next st, ch 3, sk next ch sp and 2 sts, dc in next st, ch 3, sk next 2 sts, dc in each of next 4 sts, sk next ch sp, 5 dc in next st, ch 2, sk next 4 sts] across with dc in each of last 6 sts, turn. (217 dc)

Row 26: Ch 3, dc in each of next 5 sts, sk next ch sp, 5 dc in next st, ch 2, sk next 4 sts, [dc in next st, 2 dc in next st, dc in each of next 2 sts, ch 3, dc in next st, ch 2, 5 dc in next st, ch 2, sk next 3 sts, 5 dc in next st, ch 2, dc in next st, ch 3, dc in each of next 2 sts, 2 dc in next st, dc in next st, sk next ch sp, 5 dc in next st, ch 2, sk next 4 sts] across with dc in each of last 6 sts, turn. (287 dc)

Row 27: Ch 3, dc in each of next 5 sts, sk next ch sp, 5 dc in next st, ch 2, sk next 4 sts, [dc in each of next 5 sts, ch 3, sk next ch sp, dc in next st, 5 dc in next st, ch 3, dc in next ch sp, ch 3, sk next 4 sts, 5 dc in next st, sk next ch sp, dc in next st, ch 3, dc in each of

next 5 sts, sk next ch sp, 5 dc in next st, ch 2, sk next 4 sts] across with dc in each of last 6 sts, turn. (297 dc)

Row 28: Ch 3, dc in each of next 5 sts, sk next ch sp, 5 dc in next st, ch 2, sk next 4 sts, [dc in each of next 5 sts, sk next ch sp and next st, 5 dc in next st, sk next 3 sts, 5 dc in next st, dc in next st, 5 dc in next st, sk next 3 sts, 5 dc in next st, sk next st and next ch sp, dc in each of next 5 sts, sk next ch sp, 5 dc in next st, ch 2, sk next 4 sts] across with dc in each of last 6 sts, turn. (377 dc)

Row 29: Ch 3, dc in each of next 5 sts, sk next ch sp, 5 dc in next st, ch 2, sk next 4 sts, [dc in each of next 5 sts, ch 3, sk next 2 sts dc in next st, ch 3, sk next 2 sts, dc in sp between dc-groups, ch 3, sk next 2 sts, dc in next st, sk next 2 sts, 5 dc in next st, sk next 2 sts, dc in next st, ch 3, sk next 2 sts, dc in sp between dc-groups, ch 3, sk next 2 sts, dc in next st, ch 3, sk next 2 sts, dc in each of next 5 sts, sk next ch sp, 5 dc in next st, ch 2, sk next 4 sts] across with dc in each of last 6 sts, turn. (277 dc)

Row 30: Ch 3, dc in each of next 5 sts, sk next ch sp, 5 dc in next st, ch 2, sk next 4 sts, *dc in each of next 5 sts, ch 3, [dc in next st, ch 3] 3 times, sk next 2 sts, dc in next st, ch 3, sk next 2 sts, [dc in next st, ch 3] 3 times, dc in each of next 5 sts, sk next ch sp, 5 dc in next st, ch 2, sk next 4 sts, rep from * across with dc in each of last 6 sts, turn. (237 dc)

Row 31: Ch 3, dc in each of next 5 sts, sk next ch sp, 5 dc in next st, ch 2, sk next 4 sts, *dc in next st, 2 dc in next st, dc in each of next 3 sts, ch 3, [dc in next st, ch 3] 3 times, (dc, ch 2, dc) in next st, ch 3, [dc in next st, ch 3] 3 times, dc in each of next 3 sts, 2 dc in next st, dc in next st, sk next ch sp, 5 dc in next st, ch 2, sk next 4 sts, rep from * across with dc in each of last 6 sts, turn. (267 dc)

Row 32: Ch 3, dc in each of next 5 sts, sk next ch sp, 5 dc in next st, ch 2, sk next 4 sts, *dc in each of next 6 sts, ch 3, [dc in next st, ch 3] 3 times, sk next ch sp and next st, 5 dc in next ch sp, ch 3, sk next ch sp [dc in next st, ch 3] 3 times, dc in each of next 6 sts, sk next ch sp, 5 dc in next st, ch 2, sk next 4 sts, rep from * across with dc in each of last 6 sts, turn. (297 dc)

Row 33: Ch 3, dc in each of next 5 sts, sk next ch sp, 5 dc in next st, ch 2, sk next 4 sts, *dc in each of next 6 sts, ch 3, [dc in next st, ch 3] twice, dc in next st, 3 dc in next st, sk next st, sc in next st, sk next st, 3 dc in next st, dc in next st, ch 3, [dc in next st, ch 3] twice, dc in each of next 6 sts, sk next ch sp, 5 dc in next st, ch 2, sk next 4 sts, rep from * across with dc in each of last 6 sts, turn.

Row 34: Ch 3, dc in each of next 5 sts, sk next ch sp, 5 dc in next st, ch 2, sk next 4 sts, *dc in each of next 6 sts, ch 3, [dc in next st, ch 3] 3 times, sk next 3 sts, (dc, ch 2, dc) in sc, ch 3, sk next 3 sts, [dc in next st, ch 3] 3 times, dc in each of next 6 sts, sk next ch sp, 5 dc in next st, ch 2, sk next 4 sts, rep from * across with dc in each of last 6 sts, turn.

Row 35: Ch 3, dc in each of next 5 sts, sk next ch sp, 5 dc in next st, ch 2, sk next 4 sts, *dc in each of next 6 sts, ch 3, [dc in next st, ch 3] 3 times, sk next ch sp and next st, 5 dc in next ch sp, ch 3, sk next st and ch sp, [dc in next st, ch 3] 3 times, dc in each of next 6 sts, sk next ch sp, 5 dc in next st, ch 2, sk next 4 sts, rep from * across with dc in each of last 6 sts, turn.

Row 36: Ch 3, dc in each of next 5 sts, sk next ch sp, 5 dc in next st, ch 2, sk next 4 sts, *dc in each of next 6 sts, ch 3, [dc in next st, ch 3] 3 times, 3 dc in next st, ch 2, sk next 3 sts, 3 dc in next st, ch 3, [dc in next st, ch 3] 3 times, dc in each of next 6 sts, sk next ch sp, 5 dc in next st, ch 2, sk next 4 sts, rep from * across with dc in each of last 6 sts, turn.

Row 37: Ch 3, dc in each of next 5 sts, sk next ch sp, 5 dc in next st, ch 2, sk next 4 sts, *dc in each of next 6 sts, ch 2, sk next ch sp, 5 dc in next ch sp, ch 3, sk next ch sp, [5 dc in next ch sp, ch 2] twice, 5 dc in next ch sp, ch 3, sk next ch sp, 5 dc in next ch sp, ch 3, sk next st and ch sp, dc in each of next 6 sts, sk next ch sp, 5 dc in next st, ch 2,

sk next 4 sts, rep from * across with dc in each of last 6 sts, turn.

Row 38: Ch 3, dc in each of next 5 sts, sk next ch sp, 5 dc in next st, ch 2, sk next 4 sts, *dc in each of next 6 sts, sk next ch sp, [3 dc in next st, ch 1, sk next 3 sts, 3 dc in next st, ch 1] 5 times, sk next ch sp, dc in each of next 6 sts, sk next ch sp, 5 dc in next st, ch 2, sk next 4 sts, rep from * across with dc in each of last 6 sts, turn.

Row 39: Ch 3, dc in each of next 5 sts, sk next ch sp, 5 dc in next st, ch 2, sk next 4 sts, *dc in each of next 6 sts, ch 3, [sk next 3 sts, dc in next ch sp, ch 3] 4 times, sk next 3 sts, (dc, ch 3, dc) in next ch sp, ch 3, [sk next 3 sts, dc in next ch sp, ch 3] 4 times, sk next 3 sts, dc in each of next 6 sts, sk next ch sp, 5 dc in next st, ch 2, sk next 4 sts, rep from * across with dc in each of last 6 sts, turn.

Row 40: Ch 3, dc in each of next 5 sts, sk next ch sp, 5 dc in next st, ch 2, sk next 4 sts, *dc in each of next 6 sts, ch 2, sk next ch sp, [5 dc in next ch sp, ch 2, sk next ch sp] 5 times, dc in each of next 6 sts, sk next ch sp, 5 dc in next st, ch 2, sk next 4 sts, rep from * across with dc in each of last 6 sts, turn.

Row 41: Ch 3, dc in each of next 5 sts, sk next ch sp, 5 dc in next st, ch 2, sk next 4 sts, *dc in each of next 6 sts, ch 3, sk next ch sp and next 2 sts, 5 dc in next st, [ch 2, sk next 2 sts, sc in next ch sp, ch 2, sk next 2 sts, 5 dc in next st] 4 times, ch 3, sk next 2 sts and ch sp, dc in each of next 6 sts, sk next ch sp, 5 dc in next st, ch 2, sk next 4 sts, rep from * across with dc in each of last 6 sts, turn.

Row 42: Ch 3, dc in each of next 5 sts, sk next ch sp, 5 dc in next st, ch 2, sk next 4 sts, *dc in each of next 6 sts, ch 3, sk next ch sp and next 2 sts, 5 dc in next st, [ch 3, sk next 2 sts, next ch sp, next sc, next ch sp and next 2 sts, 5 dc in next st] 4 times, ch 3, sk next 2 sts, dc in each of next 6 sts, sk next ch sp, 5 dc in next st, ch 2, sk next 4 sts, rep from * across with dc in each of last 6 sts, turn.

Row 43: Ch 3, dc in each of next 5 sts, sk next ch sp, 5 dc in next st, ch

2, sk next 4 sts, *dc in each of next 6 sts, ch 2, sc in next ch sp, ch 2, sk next 2 sts, 5 dc in next st, [ch 2, sk next 2 sts, sc in next ch sp, ch 2, sk next 2 sts, 5 dc in next st] 4 times, ch 2, sk next 2 sts, sc in next ch sp, ch 2, dc in each of next 6 sts, sk next ch sp, 5 dc in next st, ch 2, sk next 4 sts, rep from * across with dc in each of last 6 sts, turn. Fasten off.

RIGHT FRONT TRIM

Row 1: Working in ends of rows, join with sc in end of first row, sc in same row, 2 sc in each row across, turn. *(86 sc made)*

Row 2: Ch 1, sc in each st across, turn.

Row 3: Ch 1, sc in each of first 2 sts, for **buttonhole**, [ch 3, sk next 2 sts, sc in each of next 9 sts] 6 times, sc in each st across, turn.

Row 4: Ch 1, sc in each st and in each ch across, turn.

Rows 5 & 6: Ch 1, sc in each st across, turn. At end of last row, fasten off.

LEFT FRONT TRIM

Row 1: Working in ends of rows, join with sc in end of first row, sc in same row, 2 sc in each row across, turn. *(86 sc made)*

Rows 2–6: Ch 1, sc in each st across, turn. At end of last row, fasten off. Sew buttons opposite buttonholes.

NECK BAND

Row 1: Working in starting ch on opposite side of row 1, join with sc in first ch, sc in each of next 9 chs, [**sc dec** *(see Stitch Guide)* in next 2 chs] twice, [sc in each of next 10 chs, sc dec in next 2 chs] twice, [sc in each of next 9 chs, sc dec in next 2 chs] twice, [sc in each of next 10 chs, sc dec in next 2 chs] twice, sc dec in next 2 chs, sc in each of last 10 chs, turn. *(87 sc)*

Rows 2 & 3: Ch 1, hdc in first st and in each st across, turn.

Row 4: Ch 1, hdc in first st, **hdc dec** *(see Stitch Guide)* in next 2 sts, hdc in each st across to last 3 sts, hdc dec in next 2 sts, hdc in last st. Fasten off.❑❑

Evening Sonnet

Design by Melissa Leapman

SKILL LEVEL

■■■□ INTERMEDIATE

FINISHED SIZE

One size fits most

FINISHED MEASUREMENTS

Approx 59½ inches wide x 21 inches long

MATERIALS

❑ Wool Ease 78 percent acrylic/19 percent wool/3 percent polyester worsted weight yarn from Lion Brand (162 yds/2½ oz per ball): 7 balls white multi #301

[4 MEDIUM]

❑ Size 6 (4mm) 16- and 29-inch circular needles
❑ Size 7 (4.5mm) 29-inch circular needle or size needed to obtain gauge
❑ Stitch holders

GAUGE

10 sts and 26 rows = 4 inches/10cm in pat st
To save time, take time to check gauge.

PATTERN NOTE

Circular needle is used to accommodate large number of sts. Do not join; work in rows.
Slip all sts knitwise.

BACK

Beg at border with smaller needles, cast on 149 sts.

Row 1 (RS): [K1, yo, sl 2, k1, p2sso, yo, k4] 18 times; k1, yo, sl 2, k1, p2sso, yo, k1.

Row 2: Knit.

Rep Rows 1–2 until piece measures 1½ inches, ending with a WS row.

Change to larger needles.

Begin body

Row 1 (RS): Knit.

Row 2: Purl.

Row 3: *K5, p3; rep from * to last 5 sts, k5.

Row 4: *P5, k3; rep from * to last 5 sts, p5.

Row 5: *K5, yo, sl 2, k1, p2sso, yo; rep from * to last 5 sts, k5.

Row 6: Knit.

Rows 7 and 8: Rep Rows 1 and 2.

Row 9: *K1, p3, k4; rep from * to last 5 sts, k1, p3, k1.

Row 10: *P1, k3, p4; rep from * to last 5 sts, p1, k3, p1.

Row 11: *K1, yo, sl 2, k1, p2sso, yo, k4; rep from * to last 5 sts, k1, yo, sl 2, k1, p2sso, yo, k1.

Row 12: Purl.

[Rep Rows 1–12] twice; rep Rows 1–4.

Row 41: K1, ssk, k2, yo, sl 2, k1, p2sso, yo, *k5, yo, sl 2, k1, p2sso, yo; rep from * to last 5 sts, k2, k2 tog, k1–147 sts.

Row 42: Purl.

Rows 43 and 44: Rep Rows 1 and 2.

Row 45: K1, ssk, work in pat to last 3 sts, k2tog, k1—145 sts.

Rows 46–48: Work even in established pat.

Rows 49–60: [Rep Rows 45–48] 3 times—139 sts.

Row 61: K1, ssk, work in pat to last 3 sts, k2tog, k1—137 sts.

Row 62: Work even in established pat.

Row 63: K1, ssk, work in pat to last 3 sts, k2tog, k1—135 sts.

[Rep Rows 62 and 63] 18 times—99 sts.

Row 100: P1, P2tog, work in pat to last 3 sts, p2tog-tbl, p1—97 sts.

Row 101: K1, ssk, work in pat to last 3 sts, k2tog, k1—95 sts.

[Rep Rows 100 and 101] 7 times—67 sts.

Next row: Rep Row 100—65 sts.

Shape neckline

Note: *Work both sides at same time with separate balls of yarn.*

Row 1: K1, ssk, work in pat across 19 sts, slip next 21 sts to holder for neck, join 2nd ball of yarn, work in pat across 19 sts, k2 tog, k1–21 sts on each side.

Row 2: P1, p2tog, work in pat across 18 sts; on next side bind off 4 sts, work in pat to last 3 sts, p2tog-tbl, p1.

Row 3: K1, ssk, work in pat across 13 sts; on next side bind off 4 sts, work in pat to last 3 sts, k2tog, k1—15 sts on each side.

Row 4: P1, p2 tog, work in pat across 12 sts; on next side bind off 2 sts, work in pat to last 3 sts, p2tog-tbl, p1.

Row 5: K1, ssk, work in pat across 9 sts; on next side bind off 2 sts, work in pat to last 3 sts, k2tog, k1–11 sts on each side.

Row 6: P1, p2tog, work in pat across 8 sts; on next side bind off 2 sts, work in pat to last 3 sts, p2tog-tbl, p1.

Row 7: K1, ssk, work in pat across 5 sts; on next side bind off 2 sts, work in pat to last 3 sts, k2tog, k1–7 sts on each side.

Row 8: P1, p2tog, work in pat across 4 sts; on next side work in pat across next 4 sts, p2tog-tbl, p1–6 sts on each side.

Row 9: K1, ssk, k1, k2tog; on next side ssk, k1, k2 tog, k1—4 sts on each side.

row 10: P1, p2tog, p1; on next side p1, p2tog-tbl, p1–3sts on each side.

Row 11: K1, ssk; on next side k2tog, k1–2sts on each side.

Bind off purlwise.

Sew shoulder seams.

FRONT

Work as for back.

NECKBAND

Beg at seam with RS facing using smaller circular needle, pick up and knit 13 sts along neck edge, knit 21 sts from holder, pick up and knit 13 sts along neck edge to next seam, 1 st in seam, 13 sts along neck edge, knit 21 sts from holder, pick up and knit 13 sts along rem neck edge—95 sts.

Place marker between first and last st.

Rnd 1: Purl.

Rnd 2: Knit.

Rnd 3: Purl.

Rnd 4: [K7, k2tog, k8, k2tog] 5 times–85 sts.

Rnds 5–7: Rep Rnds 2–4.

Bind off knitwise.❑❑

Diamonds & Fur

Design by Belinda "Bendy" Carter

SKILL LEVEL

 INTERMEDIATE

FINISHED SIZES

Ladies 32–34-inch bust *(small)*; 34–36-inch bust *(medium)*; 36–38-inch bust *(large)*; 38–40-inch bust *(X-large)* Pattern is written for small size with larger sizes in [ ].

FINISHED GARMENT MESUREMENTS

52¾ [55, 59¾, 63] inches

MATERIALS

❑ Lion Brand Fun Fur bulky (chunky) weight yarn: (1½ oz/57 yds/40g per skein):
    5 [5, 6, 6] skeins #195 hot pink
    4 [4, 5, 5] skeins #148 turquoise
    4 [4, 5, 5] skeins #191 violet
❑ Lion Brand Wool-Ease medium (worsted) weight yarn: (3 oz/197 yds/85g per skein):
    2 [2, 2, 2] skeins #153 black
❑ Sizes J/10/6mm and K/10½/ 6.5mm crochet hooks or size needed to obtain gauge
❑ Tapestry needle
❑ 18 clear 5mm round faceted stones
❑ Aleene's Original Tacky Glue

GAUGE

Size K hook: 18 sts = 7 inches; 11 rows = 4 inches
Take time to check gauge.

COLOR & HOOK SEQUENCE

With size K hook, work 4 rows each in colors hot pink, turquoise and violet.
With size J hook, work 2 rows in black.
With size K hook, work 2 rows each in hot pink, turquoise and violet.
With size J hook, work 2 rows in black.
With size K hook, work 6 rows each in hot pink, turquoise and violet.
With size J hook, work 2 rows in black.
With size K hook, work 2 rows each in hot pink, turquoise and violet.
With size J hook, work 2 rows in black. Rep Color Sequence throughout.

INSTRUCTIONS

BACK

Row 1: With size K hook and hot pink, ch 69 [73, 79, 83], sc in 2nd ch from hook and in each ch across, turn *(first row in Color and Hook Sequence)*. (68, [72, 78, 82] sc made)

Row 2: Ch 1, sc in each st across, turn *(second row in Color and Hook Sequence)*.

Next rows: Rep row 2 following Color

and Hook Sequences until piece measures 27½ inches from beg.

Shoulder Shaping: Maintain pattern and Color and Hook Sequence, sc in each of next 26 [28, 30, 32] sts. Fasten off.

Shoulder Shaping: Sk next 16 [16, 18, 18] sts, join with sc in next st, sc in each st across. Fasten off.

FRONT

Work same as Back until piece is 20 rows less than Back.

First V-neck shaping: Keep with pattern, work next row in Color and Hook Sequence across 34 [36, 39, 41] sts, turn.

Next rows: Work 2 more rows in pattern following Color and Hook Sequence.

Next rows: Continue to work in pattern and following Color and Hook Sequence until Front is 6 rows less than Back and at the same time, **sc dec** *(see Stitch Guide)* in next 2 sts at neck edge on next row and every third row 3 times, ending with *(30, [32, 35, 37] sts)* in last row.

First neck shaping: Continue pattern and following Color and Hook Sequence until Front is same length

as Back and at the same time, sc dec in next 2 sts [2, 3, 3] times at neck edge on next row and once at neck edge on each of next 2 rows. At end of last row, fasten off.

Second V-neck & neck shaping: Following Color and Hook Sequence, join yarn in next st, rep first V-neck & neck shaping.

Sew shoulder seams.

Trim: With RS facing, join black with sc in any row, evenly space sc around, join with sl st in first sc. Fasten off.

Work Trim around neck edge, sides and bottom edges.

Ties: (Work 3 ties on each side of Front and Back for a total of 12 ties, working ties every 6 inches, starting 6 inches from bottom edge as indicated on illustration.)

With RS facing, with size J hook, join black with sl st in side, ch 25. Fasten off.

Front straps: With size J hook and black, leaving long end for sewing, make 4 straps as follows:

Ch 13, sl st in **back lp** *(see Stitch Guide)* of each ch across. Fasten off.

Ch 19, sl st in back lp of each ch across. Fasten off.

Ch 25, sl st in back lp of each ch across. Fasten off.

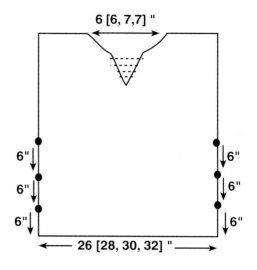

Ch 31, sl st in back lp of each ch across. Fasten off.

Mark positions for 4 straps, evenly spaced across V-neck opening 1 inch from opening edge on each side.

Insert smaller strap through first, insert end of strap through first marked opening on each side of V-neck. Fold ends of strap under and sew ends to secure.

Rep with each strap going up opening.

Glue 3 stones evenly sp across first strap, 4 stones across 2nd strap, 5 stones across 3rd and 6 stones across 4th. ❑❑

Standard Yarn Weight System
Categories of yarn, gauge ranges, and recommended needle sizes

Yarn Weight Symbol & Category Names	1 SUPER FINE	2 FINE	3 LIGHT	4 MEDIUM	5 BULKY	6 SUPER BULKY
Type of Yarns in Category	Sock, Fingering, Baby	Sport, Baby	DK, Light Worsted	Worsted, Afghan, Aran	Chunky, Craft, Rug	Bulky, Roving
Knit Gauge* Ranges in Stockinette Stitch to 4 inches	21–32 sts	23–26 sts	21–24 sts	16–20 sts	12–15 sts	6–11 sts
Recommended Needle in Metric Size Range	2.25–3.25mm	3.25–3.75mm	3.75–4.5mm	4.5–5.5mm	5.5–8mm	8mm
Recommended Needle U.S. Size Range	1 to 3	3 to 5	5 to 7	7 to 9	9 to 11	11 and larger

* GUIDELINES ONLY: The above reflect the most commonly used gauges and hook sizes for specific yarn categories.

Skill Levels

◧▭▭▭ **BEGINNER**
Beginner projects using basic stitches. Minimal shaping.

◧◧▭▭ **EASY**
Projects using basic stitches, repetitive stitch patterns, simple color changes and simple shaping and finishing.

◧◧◧▭ **INTERMEDIATE**
Projects with a variety of stitches, mid-level shaping and finishing.

◧◧◧◧ **EXPERIENCED**
Projects using advanced techniques and stitches, more intricate lace patterns and numerous color changes.

Crochet Stitch Guide

ABBREVIATIONS

beg	begin/beginning
bpdc	back post double crochet
bpsc	back post single crochet
bptr	back post treble crochet
CC	contrasting color
ch	chain stitch
ch-	refers to chain or space previously made (i.e. ch-1 space)
ch sp	chain space
cl	cluster
cm	centimeter(s)
dc	double crochet
dec	decrease/decreases/decreasing
dtr	double treble crochet
fpdc	front post double crochet
fpsc	front post single crochet
fptr	front post treble crochet
g	gram(s)
hdc	half double crochet
inc	increase/increases/increasing
lp(s)	loop(s)
MC	main color
mm	millimeter(s)
oz	ounce(s)
pc	popcorn
rem	remain/remaining
rep	repeat(s)
rnd(s)	round(s)
RS	right side
sc	single crochet
sk	skip(ped)
sl st	slip stitch
sp(s)	space(s)
st(s)	stitch(es)
tog	together
tr	treble crochet
trtr	triple treble
WS	wrong side
yd(s)	yard(s)
yo	yarn over

Chain—ch: Yo, pull through lp on hook.

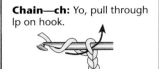

Slip stitch—sl st: Insert hook in st, yo, pull through both lps on hook.

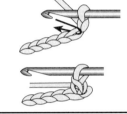

Single crochet—sc: Insert hook in st, yo, pull through st, yo, pull through both lps on hook.

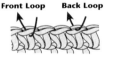

Front loop—front lp
Back loop—back lp

Front Loop   Back Loop

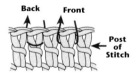

Front post stitch—fp: Back post stitch—bp: When working post st, insert hook from right to left around post st on previous row.

Back   Front

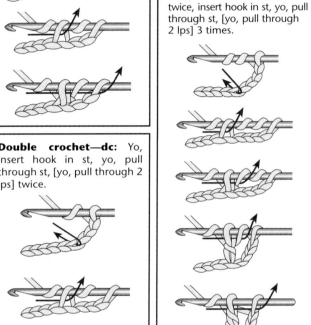

Post of Stitch

Half double crochet—hdc: Yo, insert hook in st, yo, pull through st, yo, pull through all 3 lps on hook.

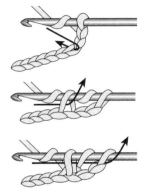

Double crochet—dc: Yo, insert hook in st, yo, pull through st, [yo, pull through 2 lps] twice.

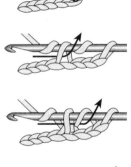

Change colors: Drop first color; with second color, pull through last 2 lps of st.

Treble crochet—tr: Yo twice, insert hook in st, yo, pull through st, [yo, pull through 2 lps] 3 times.

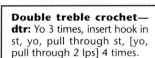

Double treble crochet—dtr: Yo 3 times, insert hook in st, yo, pull through st, [yo, pull through 2 lps] 4 times.

Single crochet decrease (sc dec): (Insert hook, yo, draw up a lp) in each of the sts indicated, yo, draw through all lps on hook.

Example of 2-sc dec

Half double crochet decrease (hdc dec): (Yo, insert hook, yo, draw lp through) in each of the sts indicated, yo, draw through all lps on hook.

Example of 2-hdc dec

Double crochet decrease (dc dec): (Yo, insert hook, yo, draw lp through, yo, draw through 2 lps on hook) in each of the sts indicated, yo, draw through all lps on hook.

Example of 2-dc dec

US		UK
sl st (slip stitch)	=	sc (single crochet)
sc (single crochet)	=	dc (double crochet)
hdc (half double crochet)	=	htr (half treble crochet)
dc (double crochet)	=	tr (treble crochet)
tr (treble crochet)	=	dtr (double treble crochet)
dtr (double treble crochet)	=	ttr (triple treble crochet)
skip	=	miss

For more complete information, visit

StitchGuide.com

Knit Stitch Guide

CAST ON

Leaving an end about an inch long for each stitch to be cast on, make a slip knot on the right needle.

Place the thumb and index finger of your left hand between the yarn ends with the long yarn end over your thumb and the strand from the skein over your index finger. Close your other fingers over the strands to hold them against your palm. Spread your thumb and index fingers apart and draw the yarn into a "V."

Place the needle in front of the strand around your thumb and bring it underneath this strand. Carry the needle over and under the strand on your index finger.

Draw through loop on thumb.

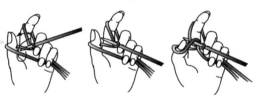

Drop the loop from your thumb and draw up the strand to form a stitch on the needle.

Repeat until you have cast on the number of stitches indicated in the pattern. Remember to count the beginning slip knot as a stitch.

CABLE CAST-ON

This type of cast-on is used when adding stitches in the middle or at the end of a row.

Make a slip knot on the left needle.

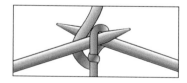

Knit a stitch in this knot and place it on the left needle.

Insert the right needle between the last two stitches on the left needle. Knit a stitch and place it on the left needle. Repeat for each stitch needed.

KNIT (K)

Insert tip of right needle from front to back in next stitch on left needle.

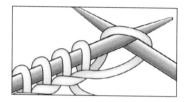

Bring yarn under and over the tip of the right needle.

Pull yarn loop through the stitch with right needle point.

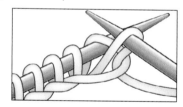

Slide the stitch off the left needle. The new stitch is on the right needle.

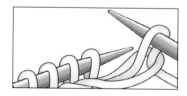

PURL (P)

With yarn in front, insert tip of right needle from back to front through next stitch on the left needle.

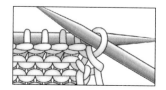

Bring yarn around the right needle counterclockwise.

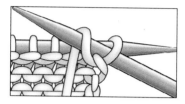

With right needle, draw yarn back through the stitch.

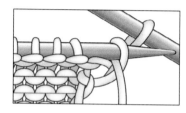

Slide the stitch off the left needle. The new stitch is on the right needle.

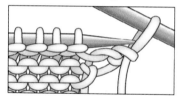

BIND OFF
Binding off (knit)

Knit first two stitches on left needle. Insert tip of left needle into first stitch worked on right needle and pull it over the second stitch and completely off the needle.

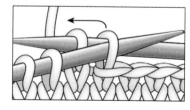

Knit the next stitch and repeat. When one stitch remains on right needle, cut yarn and draw tail through last stitch to fasten off.

Binding off (purl)

Purl first two stitches on left needle. Insert tip of left needle into first stitch worked on right needle and pull it over the second stitch and completely off the needle.

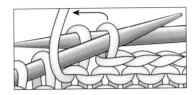

Purl the next stitch and repeat. When one stitch remains on right needle, cut yarn and draw tail through last stitch to fasten off.

INCREASE (INC)
Two stitches in one stitch
Increase (knit)
Knit the next stitch in the usual manner, but don't remove the stitch from the left needle. Place right needle behind left needle and knit again into the back of the same stitch. Slip original stitch off left needle.

INCREASE (PURL)
Purl the next stitch in the usual manner, but don't remove the stitch from the left needle. Place right needle behind left needle and purl again into the back of the same stitch. Slip original stitch off left needle.

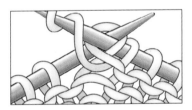

INVISIBLE INCREASE (M1)
There are several ways to make or increase one stitch.

Make 1 with Left Twist (M1L)
Insert left needle from front to back under the horizontal loop between the last stitch worked and next stitch on left needle.

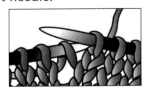

With right needle, knit into the back of this loop.

To make this increase on the purl side, insert left needle in same manner and purl into the back of the loop.

Make 1 with Right Twist (M1R)
Insert left needle from back to front under the horizontal loop between the last stitch worked and next stitch on left needle.

With right needle, knit into the front of this loop.

To make this increase on the purl side, insert left needle in same manner and purl into the front of the loop.

Make 1 with Backward Loop over the right needle
With your thumb, make a loop over the right needle.

Slip the loop from your thumb onto the needle and pull to tighten.

Make 1 in top of stitch below
Insert tip of right needle into the stitch on left needle one row below.

Knit this stitch, then knit the stitch on the left needle.

DECREASE (DEC)
Knit 2 together (k2tog)
Put tip of right needle through next two stitches on left needle as to knit. Knit these two stitches as one.

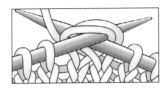

Purl 2 together (p2tog)
Put tip of right needle through next two stitches on left needle as to purl. Purl these two stitches as one.

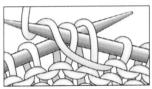

SLIP, SLIP, KNIT (SSK)
Slip next two stitches, one at a time, as to knit from left needle to right needle.

Insert left needle in front of both stitches and work off needle together.

SLIP, SLIP, PURL (SSP)
Slip next two stitches, one at a time, as to knit from left needle to right needle. Slip these stitches back onto left needle keeping them twisted.

Purl these two stitches together through back loops.

Knitting Basic Stitches

Garter Stitch
On straight needles knit every row. When working in the round on circular or double-pointed needles, knit one round then purl one round.

Stockinette Stitch
On straight needles knit right-side rows and purl wrong-side rows. When working on circular or double-pointed needles, knit all rounds.

Reverse Stockinette Stitch
On straight needles purl right-side rows and knit wrong-side rows. On circular or double-pointed needles, purl all rounds.

Ribbing
Combining knit and purl stitches within a row to give stretch to the garment. Ribbing is most often used for the lower edge of the front and back, the cuffs and neck edge of garments.

The rib pattern is established on the first row. On subsequent rows the knit stitches are knitted and purl stitches are purled to form the ribs.

READING PATTERN INSTRUCTIONS
Before beginning a pattern, look through it to make sure you are familiar with the abbreviations that are used.

Some patterns may be written for more than one size. In this case the smallest size is given first and others are placed in parentheses. When only one number is given, it applies to all sizes.

You may wish to highlight the numbers for the size you are making before beginning. It is also helpful to place a self-adhesive sheet on the pattern to note any changes made while working the pattern.

MEASURING
To measure pieces, lay them flat on a smooth surface. Take the measurement in the middle of the piece. For example, measure the length to the armhole in the center of the front or back piece, not along the outer edge where the edges tend to curve or roll.

KNITTING NEEDLES CONVERSION CHART

U.S.	0	1	2	3	4	5	6	7	8	9	10	10$\frac{1}{2}$	11	13	15
Metric(mm)	2	2$\frac{1}{4}$	2$\frac{3}{4}$	3$\frac{1}{4}$	3$\frac{1}{2}$	3$\frac{3}{4}$	4	4$\frac{1}{2}$	5	5$\frac{1}{2}$	6	6$\frac{1}{2}$	8	9	10

GAUGE
The single most important factor in determining the finished size of a knit item is the gauge. Although not as important for flat, one-piece items, it is important when making a clothing item that needs to fit properly.

It is important to make a stitch gauge swatch about 4 inches square with recommended patterns and needles before beginning.

Measure the swatch. If the number of stitches and rows are fewer than indicated under "Gauge" in the pattern, your needles are too large. Try another swatch with smaller-size needles. If the number of stitches and rows are more than indicated under "Gauge" in the pattern, your needles are too small. Try another swatch with larger-size needles.

Continue to adjust needles until correct gauge is achieved.

WORKING FROM CHARTS
When working with more than one color in a row, sometimes a chart is provided to follow the pattern. On the chart each square represents one stitch. A key is given indicating the color or stitch represented by each color or symbol in the box.

When working in rows, odd-numbered rows are usually read from right to left and even-numbered rows from left to right.

Odd-numbered rows represent the right side of the work and are usually knit. Even-numbered rows represent the wrong side and are usually purled.

When working in rounds, every row on the chart is a right-side row, and is read from right to left.

USE OF ZERO
In patterns that include various sizes, zeros are sometimes necessary. For example, k0 (0,1) means if you are making the smallest or middle size, you would do nothing, and if you are making the largest size, you would k1.

GLOSSARY
bind off—used to finish an edge

cast on—process of making foundation stitches used in knitting

decrease—means of reducing the number of stitches in a row

increase—means of adding to the number of stitches in a row

intarsia—method of knitting a multi-colored pattern into the fabric

knitwise—insert needle into stitch as if to knit

make 1—method of increasing using the strand between the last stitch worked and the next stitch

place marker—placing a purchased marker or loop of contrasting yarn onto the needle for ease in working a pattern repeat

purlwise—insert needle into stitch as if to purl

right side—side of garment or piece that will be seen when worn

selvage stitch—edge stitch used to make seaming easier

slip, slip, knit—method of decreasing by moving stitches from left needle to right needle and working them together

slip stitch—an unworked stitch slipped from left needle to right needle usually as to purl

wrong side—side that will be inside when garment is worn

work even—continue to work in the pattern as established without working any increases or decreases

work in pattern as established—continue to work following the pattern stitch as it has been set up or established on the needle, working any increases or decreases in such a way that the established pattern remains the same

yarn over—method of increasing by wrapping the yarn over the right needle without working a stitch

Knitting Standard Abbreviations

[ ] work instructions within brackets as many times as directed

( ) work instructions within parentheses in the place directed

** repeat instructions following the asterisks as directed

* repeat instructions following the single asterisk as directed

" inch(es)

approx approximately

beg begin/beginning

CC contrasting color

ch chain stitch

cm centimeter(s)

cn cable needle

dec decrease/decreases/ decreasing

dpn(s) double-pointed needle(s)

g gram

inc increase/increases/ increasing

k knit

k2tog knit 2 stitches together

LH left hand

lp(s) loop(s)

m meter(s)

M1 make one stitch

MC main color

mm millimeter(s)

oz ounce(s)

p purl

pat(s) pattern(s)

p2tog purl 2 stitches together

psso pass slipped stitch over

rem remain/remaining

rep repeat(s)

rev St st reverse stocki- nette stitch

RH right hand

rnd(s) rounds

RS right side

skp slip, knit, pass stitch over—one stitch decreased

sk2p slip 1, knit 2 together, pass slip stitch over the knit 2 together; 2 stitches have been decreased

sl slip

sl 1k slip 1 knitwise

sl 1p slip 1 purlwise

sl st slip stitch(es)

ssk slip, slip, knit these 2 stitches together—a decrease

st(s) stitch(es)

St st stockinette stitch/ stocking stitch

tbl through back loop(s)

tog together

WS wrong side

wyib with yarn in back

wyif with yarn in front

yd(s) yard(s)

yfwd yarn forward

yo yarn over

Fringe

Cut a piece of cardboard half as long as specified in instructions for strands plus ½ inch for trimming. Wind yarn loosely and evenly around cardboard. When cardboard is filled, cut yarn across one end. Do this several times then begin fringing. Wind additional strands as necessary.

SINGLE KNOT FRINGE

Hold specified number of strands for one knot together, fold in half. Hold project to be fringed with right side facing you. Use crochet hook to draw folded end through space or stitch indicated from right to wrong side.

Pull loose ends through folded section. Draw knot up firmly. Space knots as indicated in pattern instructions.

Single Knot Fringe

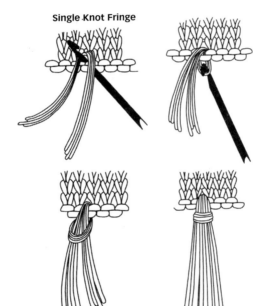

DOUBLE KNOT FRINGE

Begin by working Single Knot Fringe completely across one end of piece.

With right side facing you and working from left to right, take half the strands of one knot and half the strands of the knot next to it and knot them together.

Double Knot Fringe

TRIPLE KNOT FRINGE

Work Double Knot Fringe across. On the right side, work from left to right tying a third row of knots.

Triple Knot Fringe

Annie's Attic®

306 East Parr Road
Berne, IN 46711
© 2005 Annie's Attic

TOLL-FREE ORDER LINE or to request a free catalog (800) LV-ANNIE (800) 582-6643
Customer Service (800) AT-ANNIE (800) 282-6643, **Fax** (800) 882-6643
Visit www.AnniesAttic.com

ISBN: 1-59635-033-4   Library of Congress Control Number: 2005922470   All rights reserved   Printed in USA
1 2 3 4 5 6 7 8 9